FOREWORD

GOOSTREY'S MOST PRECIOUS resource is its inhabitan
rich community, a place where people are dedicated to enjoying life and upholding the
values which contribute towards that ethos. This book is a remarkable record of village
life stretching all the way back to the Domesday reference in 1086. It captures many
of the places, events and characters – the threads of human existence – and weaves
them into a fascinating tapestry which is both informative and pleasurable to view.
The collection of photographs has been distilled from literally thousands painstakingly
collected by my mother over many years and she acknowledges the generosity of all
who have contributed to her effort. Similarly many hours of research at libraries,
records offices and time spent talking to Goostrey residents past and present have
produced a wealth of information.

A book of this nature could never attempt to do more than offer a snapshot of the
events of the past and I think it does it very successfully. Omissions and inaccuracies
are synonymous with any historical account but I hope that the book will be judged on
what is present and correct. By any assessment the book is a testament to the theory
that being remarkable and important is often actually not that remarkable and not
that important in the grand scale of things. The start of the new millennium is a good
time to reflect on life's important qualities. In this age of rapid change and uncertainty,
constancy and continuity will become increasingly rare but ever more desirable
objectives in society. I for one will begin to relish telling people that I hail from a place
where little has changed over the years, a place where people value the important
things in life – a place called Goostrey. GR

James Smallwood
September, 2000

Published by – The Silk Press
14a Bath Street, Hale, Cheshire WA14 2EJ
Telephone: 0161 929 4884   Fax: 0161 929 8656

ISBN No: 1-902685-07-5

Layout and design: Shirley Anders, Living**EDGE** Magazine Ltd.
Covers: Goostrey yesterday and today.

ACKNOWLEDGEMENTS

My first and most important acknowledgement goes to my husband Colin, without whose encouragement, local knowledge and support this book would never have been completed. Sons James and Stewart, especially for bearing with me while I strove to master the computer; Chester Record Office; British Library London; Public Libraries in Chester, Manchester, Wilmslow and Northwich; Congleton (Sandbach) Chronicle; Mr Ian Morrison of Jodrell Bank; past and present councillors of Goostrey; Miss Mary Hooley; Mrs Margaret Kettle; Mrs Rene Kemery; Mrs Sybil Harwood; Mrs Audrey Cumberbirch; Mrs Eileen Everett; Mr Arthur Jarvis; Mr William (Bill) Lester; Mr Tom McCartney; Mr Frank Carter; Mr David Hunter; Mr Geoffrey Challinor; Mr John Knowles and so many other people who have kindly allowed me to take copies of their photographs over the past 40 years, and others who have given valuable information.

Jean Smallwood, Goostrey, November 2000

Goostrey
Remembered

by JEAN SMALLWOOD

Silk Press Books
MM

This book was published with the support of

CONTENTS

Page

5   Introduction *by Jean Smallwood*

7   The Churches: St. Luke's, Wesleyan/Methodist, Wake's Weeks

23   Listed Buildings

33   Personal Memories *by Margaret (Foden) Kettle*

37   Personal Memories *by the late Mrs Marion Hooley*

39   Other Buildings of Note

57   Inns of Character: the Crown Inn, the Red Lion Inn

63   Gooseberry Growers

67   A History of Goostrey Shops

81   Goostrey Station

85   Goostrey School

91   Personal Memories *by Arthur Jarvis*

93   Personal Memories *by Mrs Valerie Edwards*

94   Goostrey May Festival 1901

95   Goostrey Rose Festival

103   The Morris Dancers of Goostrey

105   Goostrey People and Groups

117   Goostrey Women's Institute *by Mrs Norah Relph*

123   Goostrey Sports

134   Jodrell Bank

137   Parish Council Centenary

138   Recent Developments

139   Opening the Old Footpath

140   Goostrey Tales

141   Past and Present Villagers of Goostrey

Above: Barnshaw Hall C13th. Part was a chantry chapel used by monks, circa 1249.
Medieval foundation; narrow hand-made bricks.
Below: Jodrell Bank telescope as seen from the church tower.

INTRODUCTION

FIRST MENTIONED IN the Domesday Book of 1086 under the spellings *Gostre* and *Gostrel*, this scattered village, township & chapelry in the Northwich Hundred comprised – by 1851 – 1,580 acres, 2 roods, 29 perches of land (100 acres of which in woods and plantations), had 55 houses and 268 inhabitants, of whom 143 were male and 125 female.

At this time, Henry Mainwaring Esq. was lord of the manor and owner. The heir to the title of the Lordship of Goostrey and Barnshaw, he occasionally lived at Barnshaw Hall (now divided into Cheshire County Council holdings), where there is the first definite record of religious life in the area. In the Hall was the Monks' Chapel, dated 1249, now used as a building. Some of the old marl pits that surrounded it are still visible. Also close by, the remains of barrows (ancient earth built grave mounds) have been detected and analysed, dating between 1,450BC and 1,350BC, though changes in farming make these difficult to locate. The Kinsey family, whose last male representative died in 1814 (although distant relatives still live in the area), acquired land here about 1380 by marrying one of the heiresses of the last Goostrey (family name).

The Armisteads, who provided four vicars of Goostrey and three successively from 1859 to 1923, came from Horton in Ribblesdale in the middle of the eighteenth century. Lawrence Armistead, whose memorial in Goostrey parish church is on the north wall, purchased the Cranage and Hermitage estates. The Baskervyles, whose memorials are in the north east corner of the chancel, were squires of nearby Withington from 1266 until 1954, when John Baskervyle Glegg was buried at the east end of the church, joining his ancestors.

On the south wall we read of the Booth family who lived at Twemlow Hall. This family originated in the fifteenth century at Barton near Manchester. By marriage with the Venables, they acquired Dunham Massey, and a branch by marriage with a Knutsford heiress obtained part of Twemlow when the other Knutsford heiress married a Jodrell from Yeardsley, who obtained the other part. The Jodrell heiress married Egerton Leigh from West Hall, High Leigh in 1778, and the Leigh family sold the Jodrell estate in 1924.

Today, most of the land here is owned by the families who farm it, though at the north east corner of Goostrey, Manchester University owns the land where their radio telescope overlooks the collection of neolithic barrows.

Thus in one corner of the parish space age and stone age join hands, which in one way, is what history is all about. **GR**

Population 500. Distance from Manchester, 20 miles. Trains from Manchester take 40 minutes; 11 daily and 3 on Sunday each way.

"This is a purely country district, suitable for those who desire the quietest of residences. There is good fishing in the district. There are no shopping facilities but a Post and Telegraph Office is established in the village."

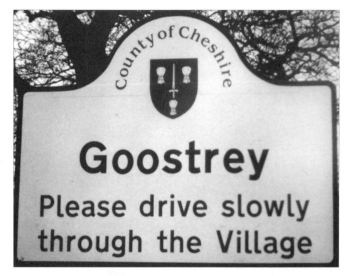

THE FOUR BOUNDARY STONES
Right: Goostrey-cum Barnshaw, close to Hawthorn cottage.
Below left: Withington (Lower)-cum-Goostrey, to the right of Hermitage Lane.
Below centre: to the left of Hermitage Lane.
Below right: Barnshaw-cum-Cranage (on private grounds).

THE CHURCHES

Above: St Luke's Church, Goostrey circa 1900. There were two pathways up to the church (one near the *Red Lion* boundary), although only one is shown here.

ST LUKE'S CHURCH

THE POSITION OF the church appears to have once formed the site of the Manor house of the "Goostre" family with its moat and drawbridge. The Church was built on the rising ground of the old Manor, exact date unknown, but records reveal that Goostrey Chapel was built before 1220, and was the first place of worship on the site. References appear in the earliest known list of diocesan churches made in connection to the tax levied by Pope Nicholas in that year. The Church pulled down before the present one was black and white, rather like Marton Church, but reported to be bitterly cold in winter and in constant need of repair. In 1711 nearly £18 was spent re-roofing for 1s.10d was spent on 3000 laths and Brooks, the slater was paid nearly £3.0s.0d and the plasterer £7.10s.0d. The Church Warden's accounts show a time when Church and State were inextricably intertwined, and everyone above the rank of cottager paid a Church rate. In 1711 it was one shilling in the pound from the whole parish which included Lees (like Barnshaw and Blackden, an old part of the parish) and £46.10s.0d was raised.

The present building was erected between 1792-1796, designed by a local brick

Above left: the Great Yew (circa 1220) near the church door.
Above centre: the C15th font.
Above right: two of the six bells in the bell tower. Climbing between bells to reach the top was difficult (but recently made easier), and has to be done to raise and lower the flag.
Centre right: the church clock mechanism supported by part of the old stocks from the Bog Bean.
Bottom right: George II's Royal Coat of Arms still in the church.
Below: Harvest Festival circa 1890.

setter. As one enters the village from the station, one sees the tall square brick tower with pinnacles, plain, built in the Norman style with a chancel, nave, and containing a clock (a part of the previous church dating 1658). The mechanism of this stands on part of the old wooden stocks that were originally on the Bog Bean in Goostrey. Another portion of the stocks is situated in the clock tower. (In 1726 the sum of four shillings was paid for the stocks). The clock is still wound twice weekly and, for an uncompensated pendulum, keeps good time (coins are added or removed to regulate and keep the correct time). There are six bells, including the original three, the first dated 1606, the heaviest weighing 6cwt. These were recast and rehung in a steel frame in 1912 and the lightest of the six bells was added at that time. Replacement to the cracked headstock of the second bell had to be dealt with in the summer of 1999.

The font dates back to the 15th century and is from the old church. It is octagonal in shape with carved quatre-foils, flowers and foliage, shields and tracery adorn the shaft. The old oak chest dates back to the 18th century. The Holy Table is 17th century. This too was saved from the old church. Also from the old church is the Royal Coat of Arms, painted and erected for £2.3s.6d. Before the first organ was installed in the 1850s, a quartet of musicians played on pianino, violin, viola & cello.

A new organ was donated in 1947 by the Goodwin family of the Orchards, Twemlow, when the pipes were moved to the gallery. This was installed by Rushworth and Draper of Chester. The problem of finding a case for the organ was solved by obtaining a suitable cabinet from Chirk Castle near Wrexham. (By the installation of the electric organ, the work of the manual organ bellow-blowers became a thing of the past). The great yew which stands in front of the porch is of enormous girth. It is known there was a church here of some kind in 1220, and in all probability the yew was present at that time, but is difficult to date accurately.

Left: the church interior, with oil lamps, organ pipes and, on either side of the altar painted in gold lettering, the Ten Commandments, the Lord's Prayer and the Creed.

Above left: Bi-centennial celebrations at St. Luke's.
Above right: the Church in 1931, with oil lamps at the gate and up the drive. Electricity came in 1934.
Centre right: Rev. W. H. Bolton (seated centre) with the choir in 1947.
Bottom right: the new Vicarage was completed in 1940 and Rev. W. H. Bolton was the first incumbent.
Below: Dedication of the new Vicarage by the Bishop of Chester.

A thorn shoot from Glastonbury, Somerset was presented by Canon Vale (vicar of Church Hulme) to the vicar of Goostrey and planted in the old churchyard opposite the war memorial in the presence of Goostrey school children on the Festival of St Michael & All Angels, in 1942.

The Stained Glass Windows

These are Victorian but not English and the probability is France or Belgium. One in memory of Mary Armistead who died in 1868. The East Window is a memorial to Egerton-Leigh Esq of Jodrell Hall, who died 3rd October 1865.

Painted round the altar in gold lettering, beautifully done, was the Lords Prayer, the Ten Commandments, and the Creed. Sadly – or so many of the older residents think – they were painted over and the walls left plain.

According to the March 1911 church magazine, many scathing but not undeserved criticisms have been passed upon the sketch – or what was formerly a sketch– of the church on the front page of the magazine. It is even said to resemble a decayed "family vault" more than the church and we are bound to confess that this is not far from the truth. The plate was specially engraved for us years ago at a cost of 14s. At first it was excellent, but its life of usefulness has been a short one. The magazine is not exactly

Below: Church and Vicarage 1928 – the ivy was removed in the 1950s. Built in 1812, this was the front view of the Vicarage until the new road was made down Church Bank (now the rear view).

Above left: the inscription beneath the church clock (now worn away) read *"Rebuilt anno domini 1792, vicar Thos. Burroughs, church wardens John Kinsey, Thos. Haselhurst".*
Above right: six bell ringers with Mr Gibbons, team leader).
Centre right: the Saltersford school band (Home Office Reform) played at various functions in the village.
Bottom right: candidates walk to church for their Confirmation Service.

run at a profit. Mrs Glazebrook, however, has kindly taken pity on us and promised to present us with a new one, so that the blurred smudge shall no longer disfigure our front page. The report of March 1913 tells of Mrs & Miss Claypole presenting the church with new violet hangings, altar cloth, curtains, book marks etc, which have been in use during Lent.

In April 1915, the plea went out for a new flag for the church - "and indeed it is essential, as the present one is in rags. We shall need one for the Bishop's visit for the Confirmation on May 18 and we earnestly hope that we shall need one still more before long, for the celebration of the Victory of Britain & Allies and the restoration of Peace. Will anyone be so kind as to present to the church or contribute to the purchase of a new St George flag? The cost would only be about £1."

In 1932 Mrs Lydia Smallwood took on the duties of caretaker and clerk and her list of duties included:-

Opening and closing of Church daily. Bellringing for all services. Clean and dust weekly. Sanctuary Floor washed each month. Spring clean once a year and after Harvest Festival.

Heating: Lighting of fire and heating of Church from Harvest to Easter and order and store coke and firewood for furnace.

Raising Flag: Raise and lower flag for Christmas, Easter and Whit-Sunday also as may be required for any special occasions.

Church Clock: To attend to the winding – three times weekly.

Attend Services: To be present at all services including baptisms, marriages and funerals.

Lighting etc: Trim all lamps and fill with oil, and light prior to evening services and 8.30 am service.

All books to be collected and lights extinguished prior to locking up after all services.

War Memorial: Clean prior to Armistice Service, Easter and Rose Festival.

Altar Linen and Surplices: Wash and Launder as required, also the Vicar's Surplice.

To receive notices of Baptisms, Banns of Marriage and Funerals.

All for £15 per annum. 15th June 1932 (post held until 1949)

In the Crypt lay the old lead coffins and remains of various gentry. These were removed to a specially prepared site in the cemetery in 1998.

Also in 1998 someone stole the lovely old gates leading into the cemetery. They were missing for almost two months, when by sheer good fortune two of the Luke brothers, who used to live in Goostrey, were looking round a builders' merchants site towards Chester, and spotted and recognised the gates for sale. They reported the sighting to the Goostrey Church Wardens, who confirmed that they were missing gates. They are now back where they belong, in their sacred place, having been made more secure. The Wheeled Bier, used for many years at funerals, was kept in a shed at the local school for many years. Dry rot, woodworm and rust put an end to it in the 1940s or 1950s. **GR**

A LIST OF INCUMBENTS, ST LUKES CHURCH, GOOSTREY

1220	Abel	1692	—-Nabbs
1244	Hugh	1693	Hugh Jennings
1320	Geoffrey de Cranach	1697	— Brooke
Circa 1548	James Brook	1699	Robert Johnson
Circa 1564	James Whytacres	1706	Cornelius Edwards
Circa 1576	Alexander Button	1707	John Harwar
Circa 1588	Thomas Waynewright	1716	William Webster
Circa 1591	John Kell	1720	John Latham
Circa 1594	John Stathom	1723	Abraham Blackshaw
Circa 1611	Thomas Wood	1735	John Hulse BA
Circa 1615	Thomas Carter	1754	Simon Mills MA
Circa 1616	John Bowen	1759	Thomas Burrows BA
Circa 1617	Joseph Becke	1809	John Armistead
Circa 1622	Richard Lingard	1814	Robert Litler
Circa 1634	William Hoult	1832	Richard Massie MA
Circa 1645	Zachary Crofton	1836	William Henry Massie BA
Circa 1648	George Eccles	1848	William Edward Dickson MA
Circa 1648	Henry Newcombe MA	1859	John Richard Armistead MA
Circa 1653	Thomas Edge	1860	William Geo Armistead MA
1657	Edward Mainwaring	1907	Edward Armistead MA
1660	John Buckley	1923	Auberon Elstob BA
1661	John Worthington	1930	Walter Henry Bolton
1663	John Buckley	1964	Albert Ashden Hughes
1667	John Yarwood	1976	Cyril Howard Huggill
1671	John Alcock	1986	Anthony George Sparham
1685	John Barker	1997	Geoffrey Buchan
1687	Edmund Hough	1999	Peter Charles Robinson

FORMER METHODIST MINISTERS

Rev C Dibnah, Rev Norris Roscoe, Rev B Owen, Rev G Roberts, Rev G Lockett, Rev F G Bourne, Rev A Middlehurst, Rev E Bagguley, Rev I Hall, Rev F Fox, Rev M Wray, Rev M Jackson, Rev D Bowker 1999

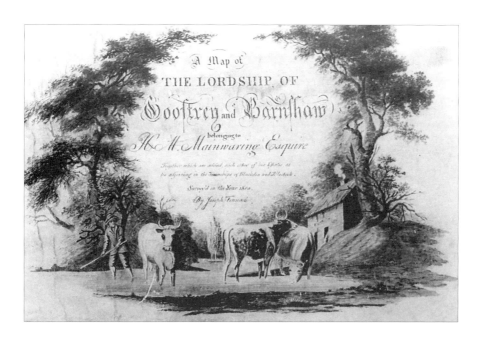

Above: A Map of THE LORDSHIP OF GOOSTREY and BARNSHAW
belonging to *H. M. Mainwaring Esquire*
Together which are added such other of his estates as be adjoining in the
townships of Blackden & Allostock. Survey'd in the year 1800 by Joseph Tennard.
Below: a sketch by the Rev. W H Massie of the church and forge in 1846.

Above: Bridge House Wesleyan Meeting House.
Below: an aerial view with the Wesleyan Chapel to the right and Bank View to the left with newspaper and grocers shops centre.

Above: the Wesleyan Chapel, which became the Methodist Church in 1932. Numerous alterations have occurred since, including the removal of the trees to the front.

GOOSTREY WESLEYAN/METHODIST CHURCH

THE FIRST MEETINGS of the Methodist members were held at Bridge House down Church Bank. Meetings were also held in other houses.

In 1875, the Wesleyan Church was built in Main Road, a Trust having been formed with eleven members, who bought a plot of land on Main Road. Subscriptions and collections raised sufficient money to pay for the building and interior fittings, plus the harmonium. The Superintendent Minister for the new church was the Reverend A Burgess.

At first, the only income to provide for the new church was from the rent of the pews. This amounted to £6 in 1877. From 1889, a small yearly sum came from the use of the vestry for a Rachabite Tent meeting. The donation was £1 and continued at this rate until 1969 (the last entry in the accounts under this heading). In 1897 the collections from the Chapel Anniversary Services were given to the Trust and a few years later proceeds of the Harvest Festival and sale of produce were added. In these early years the annual budget averaged approximately £10.

The Trust was re-formed and new Trustees appointed in 1901, 1929, 1952 and 1969. In 1969 there were sixteen members, nine of whom were women.

Above: building of the Methodist Sunday school commenced in June 1955. The foundation stone was laid by W. Lester, A. Hickson and A. Kennedy.
Below: celebrating the opening of the building are: (back row left to right) T. Hulme, W. Lester, H. Love, A. Burgess, Mrs Walton, G. Hulme, Mr Walton (Mayor [of Congleton]), D. Carter, Mrs Broom, Dr Palmer, Mrs Lester, T. Carter, Mrs Grimsditch, L. Grimsditch; (front row seated left to right) Mrs Lace, Mrs Hulme, E. Mee, Mrs Palmer, Mrs Burgess and Mrs Bates.

The great upheaval of two world wars made little impression in the Trust accounts, or the Minutes. 6/- was spent on Aircraft Insurance in 1916, reduced to 3/- in 1917/18. Telesia for making blinds was bought in 1916 and made up by members.

In 1932 the building became known as Goostrey Methodist Church.

On 13th January 1939, a Christmas party and concert were held in the Village Hall on Saturday in connection with the Methodist Church Sunday School. A Christmas tree was stripped of its gifts by Miss Summerfield and Miss Platt, the tree being lent by Rev W H Bolton. The children's prizes were presented by Miss Sproston. Mr Mee kindly gave oranges and sweets to the children. Ladies in charge of tea were Mrs Rooks, Miss Summerfield, Miss Hurstfield and Miss M Davies. A sketch was given by Miss B and Miss J Platt, Miss E Capper, Miss B Mee and Mr H Maddock. Mr Rook thanked all helpers on behalf of the church.

On 31st March 1939 a jumble sale was held in the village hall for the Methodist Church funds. Stalls were in charge of the following: Jumble, Messrs Rooks, Broome, Platt, Capper, Lever and Miss B Platt. Cakes, M/s Sproston and Wrench. Produce, Mrs Mee, Miss B Mee and Mrs Kennerley. New goods, Miss Summerfield. Remnants, Miss J Platt. Bagatelle, Miss Hurstfield. Fishing pond, Mrs T Hulme, Miss Davies. Refreshments, M/s Summerfield, Whitehurst and Lever. Stewards, Mr Rook and Mr Kennerley. More than £18 was raised towards the organ fund and cost of redecorating the Church.

In 1941, during the Second World War, War Damage Insurance was taken out. In 1945 a donation of £10 was made to the Methodist Church Fund for the rebuilding of war damaged churches. Hanging in the vestry is photographic evidence of a gathering to celebrate the Golden Jubilee in 1925.

Renovation of the Chapel took place in 1930, to the door on the North face, the stove was taken out and put in a "stoke-hole". Heating pipes were installed and the gallery "taken down and set almost on a level". The Chapel was reopened on 2nd September 1930 by Mrs Saunders of Northwich, the service being conducted by the Reverend H J Saunders. Whilst the Chapel was out of use, services were held in the Village Hall. This work cost more than the original building and it is noteworthy that as the whole sum had not been raised, the Trustees did not go to the Bank, but dug deep into their own pockets, making interest free loans so that the builder could be paid. These accounts were cleared by April 1932.

In 1931 the Sunday School presented linoleum for the floor of the renovated Chapel. The choir presented the Communion table and chair.

In 1934, electric lighting was installed. A special service was held for the "switch on" ceremony. In 1935 the Church obtained a licence for marriages and the first wedding took place in December 1935, between Miss May Davies and Mr T Hulme.

The next expansion was the building of the Sunday School, after years of saving

Above: Methodist outing to the seaside circa 1937.
Below: 1963 infants. Due to new houses and the overcrowding of the old school, the infants class was housed in the Methodist Hall.

this dream was realised. Between 1940 and 1953 the fund reached £1500. The foundation stone was laid in June 1955. The building comprised hall, kitchen and cloakrooms, and was opened on 17 September 1955. Further improvements include a brick porch at the north door (1963), an oil-fired boiler and water heating extension to the Sunday School (1966-7) also a brick extension giving a smaller room south of the Hall (1974).

Goostrey Village School held a class in the Sunday School Hall very soon after completion, due to many new houses being erected in the village and the local primary school unable to cope with the extra intake of children. A pre-school playgroup has used the building on weekdays since 1967.

Sharing in the village life by providing accommodation for many village activities means that there is in Goostrey a good feeling of neighbourliness and a real sense of belonging to the village, thanks to the generations of faith and dedication of the members. GR

WAKES WEEKS

"Ask not the reason where it did spring, for you know very well - it's an old ancient thing"

ANNUAL WAKES WEEKS, once celebrated throughout Britain, were Parish festivals held on the anniversary of the church's consecration or on the feast day of its Saint. They were so called because the parishioners "Waked" or watched in Church on the eve of the festival, and the congregation summoned at midnight by lads, who ran through the streets wearing belts hung with bells which were supposed to jangle, represented the clanging of Saint's chains.

Besides a holiday from school, potato picking week, events such as rush bearing, dancing in village rooms, annual or half yearly rents due (non payment could mean loss of tenancy) bear baiting and general feasting took place, the days sometimes ending with much drunkenness, the result of home brewed beers and wine, plus visits to local inns.

Many events took place in the village, especially at Racecourse Wood in Northwich Lane, Goostrey, on common land. Bowling for a pig, racing pigs, horse events, also weight lifting, wrestling, throwing of horse shoes, tea drinking and numerous other fun games.

The Vicar in those days (1814-32) was R Litler and either he, or a later incumbent, put a stop to the Wakes celebrations due to much drunkenness. A custom of making FERMETRI was continued for many years after. It consisted of boiled wheat grains placed in the hot oven, the swollen grain was then covered by hot milk with spices

Right the interior of the Methodist Church.

added. Some farmers wives kept up a custom of not gathering in the sheaves of corn until the Church bells rang for three Sundays.

The harvest festival services, a great feature of village life, were held annually on the second Sunday in October. The church would be decorated the previous Saturday with fruit, vegetables, corn and flowers. Ladies of the parish would also offer home-made cakes and loaves of bread, and the local baker would provide a loaf in the shape of a wheat sheaf. A childrens' service, held on the Sunday afternoon, opened with them presenting their baskets of fruit, eggs and preserves at the Altar. These gifts were sent to local hospitals, or elderly people in the village. Apart from singing hymns suitable for the occasion, the choir would have rehearsed a special anthem for all such festival days of the year.

On each Monday evening after a festival a whist drive and dance would be held. Admission for whist at 7.30pm cost 1/6d, while the dance from 10pm until the early hours would cost 2/6d. Spot prizes were awarded to couples (standing on a selected spot) when the music was ordered to stop. Pass out tickets created something of a problem for re-admission later.

One old Goostrey tradition, which petered out in the 1950s, was the roping of newly married couples, as they walked to their vehicle from the Church gate. Well wishers would stretch a rope across, expecting a coin or two from the 'groom' as a token of good luck. Also the local chimney sweep would appear in his apparel to kiss the bride and wish the couple good luck, long life and happiness.

From early Protestant times, festivals still remain strong, especially in the countryside, like the wearing of an oak leaf on 29 May (Oak Apple day), pancakes on Shrove Tuesday and April Fools Day etc. *GR*

LISTED BUILDINGS

Above left: Blackden Hall. C16th with alterations and additions, 2 storeys and attic, 3 windows including various gables, timber framed former hall, now farmhouse, with ornamental timbers, and cants at first floor and at gable. Some walls are rebuilt in brick. Interior. Stopped bevelled beams. Wide boarded doors with old strap hinges on lugs. Plain stairs. 8-panel Jacobean doors with butterfly hinges. Timber cross-framing. In Ormerod's *History of Cheshire*.

Below left: some of the very old outbuildings at Blackden Hall.

Above right: School House. C16th. 2-storey 3-window framed brick-nogged former school house, painted black and white, with front rebuilt in brown brick in 1793. Tile roof. Interior. Bevelled beams including above wide fireplace. Shaped head of doorway. Timber cross framing. Important position and association.

Below right: Toad Hall, Blackden. C16th. Cruck cottage with alterations and additions, 2-storeys and loft, 3-windows, generally timber framed, but with south wall built in brick. Brown brick stacks. Formerly thatched now with sheeting. Casements, some altered. Interior. Cruck timbers, with ties, commence at 1st floor. Square ridge, set on edge. Ledged door with old strap hinges on lugs. Now owned by the renowned writer Alan Garner (including the mud, ditches, ponds and badgers!).

Above left (1910) and below (1930): Blackden Manor dates from 1597. Timber framed mansion 2-storeys and attic, 3-windows, with added brick and stone casing and with modern wings to north. Massive brick stack with chevron brick ornament. Old flag roof. Interior. Timber framing exposed. Bevelled beams and cross beams. Stone paving (some slate). Oak panelled room with bolection moulded, raised and fielded panels. 2-panel doors with H hinges with straps. Massive oak stairs up to first floor, with ball finials to newels and turned balusters on close string. Slender staircase to attic with original framing and purlins.

Above: Dromedary Lodge, farmhouse. The pool was filled in 45 years ago.
Below: Crook Hall. C16th. late 2 storey and attic 5 window red brick farmhouse with 3 gables to south and end gables (some with timber framing remaining). Flag roof on original timbers. Near flush casements, some altered, some filled in. Thin bricks. Flues diagonally set. Narrow band at window heads, curving above windows. Cross boarded and studded entrance doors. Interior. Unusual staircase with spiral turned balusters on close string, moulded rail and square newels with oval finials. Many Tudor panelled doors stopped bevelled beams, attic stair balustrade has shaped pierced balusters.

Above: Woodwards Cottage, Mill Lane. Now burned down and demolished
(sited opposite the new footpath to Booth Bed).
Below: Mill House, Mill Lane. C18th. Altered red brick millhouse.

Above (1889) and below (1935): The Corn Mill, Mill Lane became a cheese store in 1935, then made into a private house in early 1970. The interior was just two rooms when the Pownalls bought it, plus four and a half acres of land, the mill stream, a pond and woodland. From the road it appears to be a two-level building, but from the garden its four levels can be seen. There has been a water mill on the site since C14th.

Above: Keeper's Cottage, Winterbottom. 1670.
Below: Swanwick Hall. C17th. A much altered red brick farmhouse.

Above: Millpool with Barnshaw Bank Farm top left.
Below: The old weir and sluice gate, Mill Lane. This controlled the force of the water through to the mill wheel.

Above: The Bog Bean and Main Road –
this was once a very wet bog.
Left: Bogbean (*Menyanthes trifoliata*). A
hairless creeping perennial of wet places,
sometimes forming large floating mats.
Grows in wet bogs and fens or other
shallow water. Leaves are trifoliate, on
erect stalks with obviate leaflets. Star-
shaped flowers carried in spike-like heads,
pink to pale white (flowers April to July).
The fruit is a globular capsule. The present
Bog Bean is a tidy, well-kept part of the
village and planted with several trees and
flowers, plus a seat.

Above: Cornbrook House became The Grange in Station Road. Farm and stables
Below: Buckbeam Farm cottage on the Main Road. Much altered.

PERSONAL MEMORIES

BLACKDEN HEATH FARM
by Margaret (Foden) Kettle

IN THE 1920s a family called Jervis lived here. It was only a small cottage with a water pump in the back yard and the usual toilet down the garden. About eight acres of land and a big orchard, with two pigsties and a shippon for about four cows and loose boxes. Mrs Jervis used to make butter. The eggs from the hens and spare produce that she had from the garden would also be taken to Knutsford to sell - a good ten miles round trip. Her only way to get there was to walk, carrying a huge basket. The basket was no lighter coming home, for she would buy whatever she needed while she was there. One of her sons, Jack, used to be employed by my father. Our farm (Roadside Farm) was about 300 yards from their smallholding.

Jack was well named and rather lazy, didn't like getting up in the morning, Dad used to have to go lots of times and shift him out. He was a pleasant man but very easy going, liked a bet and a pint, smoked a pipe, Erinmore tobacco I remember. It used to smell gorgeous, even from a distance away, but constantly having a pipe in his mouth didn't do much for his teeth, which were brown and misshapen. Although Mrs Jervis had such a hard life, she lived to quite a great age but lost her sight before the end of her life.

One of my chores when I got home from school would be to take her some tea, especially if Jack was working late in the harvest and such. I was a little afraid, as a young girl, for when one knocked at the door you could hear the old lady shout, "Who is it?" and then the tap-tapping of the little wooden cane she carried to guide herself along to the back door. It always seemed very dark inside and I would have to go in and put her tea on the table. The only light would be the glow from the coal fire, or oil lamps or candles, but I always admired a pair of big brass candlesticks which glowed in the dim light and which, when Mrs Jervis died, were left to my mother.

Opposite a beautiful little wood of about ten acres was Woodside cottage, occupied by the Brown family. Grace and Alice, their daughters, went to Goostrey School (Mr Brown was a driver for the once famous Bouts removal firm of Manchester). There were also few acres of land with this dwelling. Nearly every place in this area was more or less self-sufficient, with some hens, a pig and home grown fruit and vegetables.

Rabbit catching, known as Ferreting Days would take place in the winter months. A party of people with guns and ferrets would be invited to our farm one week and other farms another week, to go "rabbiting". This helped to keep the rabbit population down, otherwise there were too many and they could ruin a field of swedes or corn shoots in no time. This was before myxomatosis destroyed a lot of rabbits. There was nothing more delicious than home-made rabbit pie but now, after the disease hit them, I cannot fancy it. It was a very enjoyable pastime for the men but a busy time for the ladies, who were expected to put on food: hunks of bread and cheese for lunch, often the butter would be made by the ladies using a butter churn and the cheese would most likely be made at Crook Hall Barnshaw, by Mrs Alice Hocknell, my mother's aunt. After the shoot, a meal would be prepared, followed by a game of cards until the early hours.

(Mr Green of Blackden Hall related a similar story, when he was paid a visit by the late Mrs Wm Grimsditch and on seeing the old refectory table still in place, related that it brought back memories of her childhood view when not an inch of table could be seen, as the table was covered completely with food "nearly reaching the ceiling", there being a rabbiting party expected there to be fed.)

One of the small fields at Woodside Cottage was prone to flooding in the winter, so as soon as it became covered with ice, the children and young folk had a great time, skating and playing ice hockey during their dinner break. The water was only shallow so no one came to any harm even if the ice cracked. Winters seemed more severe then. One of my main jobs would be to clear the snow from round the hen cotes and carry sheaves of corn for the hens to scratch around in and keep them busy.

Water was always a problem, for all the water had to be pumped up from a well in the orchard. Very often it would take ages to get the pump to start up. One would have to prime it to get it going. This had to be done very often as the big tank soon became empty. It is not often nowadays that one sees icicles hanging from spouts etc and the byroads would be deep ruts of frozen snow for days on end, making travelling very difficult.

At the top of Jodrell Bank is Jodrell Hall. This was the home of Sir Edwin and Lady Stockton, now known as Terra Nova School. Will Carling, England's Rugby team captain in the 1995 World Cup Squad was educated at Terra Nova. Next to the school is Broadway Farm, now the home of the Sharpley family. Goostrey Horse Races were held here at one time, after being held at Blackden Manor. Charlie Curbishley, who was a porter at Goostrey station, took over Blackden Manor Farm and started the Twemlow Shire Horse breeding. This is still carried on by his family, Nigel Bayley and his grand-daughter Hazel Gordon, who is a Judge of these beautiful creatures at the various shows.

Turning right at Twemlow Green, where on the corner stands the old Smithy (occupied for many years by the Sweatman family). Going over the main railway line from Crewe to Manchester, times have changed. No porter or station master these days, but in 1894 there was a staff of six and steam trains were the transport then.

Goods trains were shunted about in the station yard to unload coal, which Teddy Kennerley and his daughters would then put into bags from out of the rail truck and deliver it to the surrounding area with a horse and cart.

Percy Williams of Barnshaw Hall was a big grower of rhubarb and flowers. Scabious were his main crop, he grew acres of them which looked wonderful when they were fully out, so of course he used the railway to get his produce into Manchester market quickly. In 1920, when my father first started farming, he had to take the milk to the station to catch the milk train like all the other farms, making the station a very busy place.

My grandmother on mother's side had eight children, so to ease her life a little, my mother Annie Hocknell, when she was three years old, went to Crook Hall, Barnshaw. She used to tell me how she would look out for her father coming to see her. I think she must have loved him very much. She would shout "Jonny's coming". He died quite young, about 44, I believe. Mother's grandma took her in hand and she attended Goostrey School when Mr Duckworth was headmaster. She loved meeting people and got on well with everyone who met her. Her gift for hard work never left her either.

Crook Hall is a very beautiful old house, with a three gabled frontage, a stone flag roof and two 'monkey trees' (we call them) on either side of the garden path at the front of the house. Inside the old part of the house are oak beams and thick solid oak doors which weigh a ton! I remember there used to be back stairs, but these have long gone. Attics and cellars and a terrific pantry with stone slabs all round where the food could be stored. This was in the middle of the house and was always very dark and cold.

Then there was the cheese making room at the back of the house, in which was a huge cheese vat. The milk was poured into this and brought up to a certain temperature and rennet added which caused the milk to solidify. When it was the right texture it was cut into slices one way with a huge cutter and then the opposite way to cut into cubes. As this was going on the vat was slightly tilted so that the whey drained away from the curds of cheese. The whey ran into a tank outside the cheese room and was fed to the pigs, so you see, nothing was wasted.

Between the pantry and the cheese room was the press house, where the presses stood, which were about 6 feet tall. The wooden cheese vats, which were about 2 feet across and 18 inches high, were lined with cloth and filled with the cheese curds as full as possible, to squeeze every drop of whey out. This process would take a few days and then the cheese would be tipped out and the old cloth taken off and new cheese cloth pasted all over the cheese. They would then have to stand in the cold pantry until they were mature enough to eat.

People's tastes vary. Some like the sweet crumbly taste of new cheese and others like a more mature taste, so some would be kept longer. To test how the cheese was going on, a kind of hollow skewer was pushed in, which brought out a sliver of cheese when pulled out again, which you looked at and sniffed or tasted, then it could be pushed back into the hole again and sealed up. Of course all this activity caused quite a mess and it all had to be cleaned and scrubbed until the old flag floors were nearly white. There was a wash-house quite near the house with a couple of copper boilers for heating all the water required for all this cleaning, then everywhere looked like a new pin.

John Bloor is now farming Crook Hall, but these days farming is so mechanised, instead of having a dozen or so men to run the place, he does it nearly on his own, with the help of casual labour and hiring contract people in the harvesting time. The house is very much the same as in the old days, but the cheese room has gone and in its place is a modern kitchen.

There is still a big pond with fish and a nice orchard and an outside toilet block which is being put up. The man who was doing the job had to consult Granny as to how big it had to be and she told him to widen the door and make it so that she could turn round in it with about 3 or 4 seats, very luxurious wooden ones of course, in line with holes and pans underneath. It may have been converted to water now but the building is still there. Granny called it the 'Hockey' and it had to be scrubbed until the seats were as white as snow and all the flag floors scrubbed on hands and knees then 'donkey stoned' (whitened) in a pattern round them.

In those days there was a tax charged on the number of windows in a building, so to avoid paying some of this, some windows were bricked up and a "window" painted on the wall outside. This was done at Crook Hall and now some alterations have been done and one of the windows opened up again. When the bricks were knocked out the original window frame was still there but eaten away with woodworm.

Hitler's bombers tried to alter the look of it but failed. A string of bombs were dropped during the Manchester blitz, which landed very close to Crook Hall, in a field known as Gorse Field. There was a huge crater in which a two-storey house would have fitted, only two fields away from Crook Hall and Roadside Farm, where I lived at the time. The annual Fur & Feather whist drive was in progress in the village hall at the time. We finished playing in a nervous state, made our way home carefully on our bikes in the dark, not knowing where they had landed. That same night my uncle Harry Wrench's farmhouse was completely destroyed by a direct hit and his sister and eldest son were killed. In 1918 and onwards, new council holdings were built, so that any returning personnel from the war could start up in horticulture or farming etc. **GR**

PERSONAL MEMORIES

GOOD OLD DAYS
by the late Mrs Marion Hooley

IT WAS IN the summer of 1899 that I was christened at St Luke's Church, where my forebears had worshipped for at least 230 years. Goostrey, as I remember it, was a quiet little village, the school having only a dedicated headmaster (Mr Robert Duckworth), who was choirmaster and music master as well, and one assistant, and yet we children had a good upbringing for which we thank them. It was a truly rural village life circling round the many farms and the two public houses which were farms as well.

Life started early in the morning with the rumble of the horses and carts taking the milk in large churns to the station for the 7 o'clock train, and then returning with the empty tankards. Transport was limited to bicycles, horseback and the pony and trap. A shop came to the village once a year to supply clothes, the money being collected weekly at Sunday School by the vicar.

When we first had a Rose Festival in 1907, I was chosen as Queen because I was the only girl having a white frock. Public entertainment was very sparse, there being a lovely harvest home tea followed by a dance in the school. Later, when there were two whist drives a year, we had to borrow tables from households and of course they had to be returned next morning to the respective dwellings. If we wished to visit a show in Manchester at night, we had to leave the train at Chelford because the train stopped there to pick up mail but not at Goostrey.

We had a corn mill where the farmers took their wheat to be stone ground, and the end product was home-baked. Spread with home-made farm butter, it was delicious. There was skating in the winter on the various ponds and we followed the hounds on bicycles.

There were two bakers shops in the village yet none today. There was a tailor whose suits were long wearing but not the latest styles. At one time there was a butchers shop, but meat was delivered weekly by trap from Holmes Chapel and Congleton. We possessed a wheelwright, a blacksmith, a tinker and an undertaker. At the other end of life a christening was a great event, as was a wedding, there being two dressmakers in the village. The needy were catered for:- there was soup etc supplied by the vicarage and Hall.

One celebrated Goostrey lady went round to collect when the old cow died, to purchase a new one. A request came later for false teeth "just a few for the front, no need to open your mouth as wide as a barn door" her father said! There was a wakes in the fall when we ate "fermetri", a kind of porridge spiced and baked in the oven. The maids and some of the male employees were engaged by the year, which started on New Years Day.

There was a Post Office of sorts in someone's parlour, but there were few new houses till after the war. Sanitation was poor but as yet we knew nothing better. The war years were very hard and we lost rich and poor alike. Each soldier received a parcel at Christmas which, among other goodies, contained home-made cake. We made large ones at our house and cut them in four portions, one for each soldier or sailor. We had a good peace celebration.

Goostrey has changed, there being eight hundred or more houses now, but there is much to be said for the "Good Old Days". *GR*

Above: Rees Bros. pickers at work.

OTHER BUILDINGS OF NOTE

Above: Jodrell Hall, a spacious brick mansion one mile east of Goostrey Church. It became Terra Nova Preparatory School in 1939 when the school moved from Birkdale. In 1940 school fees were 50 guineas inclusive and there were 67 boarders. The school has since expanded.
Below: workmen at Jodrell Hall in the 1920s.

Above: Twemlow Hall was formerly moated and stands on the brow of a hill commanding romantic views of the surrounding district.
Below: The Smithy, Twemlow Lane End. The "stop" sign on the road frequently changed. The road ahead was to Holmes Chapel but now a left then a right turn is required.

Above: The Orchards, Twemlow in 1988. The Brown family bought the Orchards and did away with the fruit farm, concentrating on prize-winning cattle.
Below: Orchards' fruit farm workers, 1937.

Above: George Capper ploughing at The Orchards – making way for wartime vegetables which were grown between the fruit trees.
Below: C17th Hollins Farm.

Above: Hawthorn Cottage – a preservation order has put an end to development at present.
Below: Pear Tree Cottage, Pear Tree Lane, 1895. The two cottages became one in the late 1890s.

Above: Booth Bed Lane in 1948 – before housing development on the right hand side.
Below: Appleton's Lane (turn right near the end of Booth Bed Lane into Red Lane through to Barnshaw).

Above: Booth Bed Lane cottage – demolished in the early 1900s.
Below: Brick Bank cottage, Booth Bed Lane.

Above: part of Wood Lane towards Harrison Drive and **Right:** between Harrison Drive and Brick Bank Lane. This was known as Monks' Walk. The monks used it when walking to Chester.

Above: Dribbles or Ribbles Bridge. Ribbles Bridge cottage was flooded when a dam burst above Macclesfield due to storms. The family was rescued through the bedroom window. No sign of the cottage remains. Date unknown.
Below: C18th. Shawcroft Hall, a listed building.

Above: the Old Medicine House (© Congleton Chronicle). This was moved from Wrinehill for writer Alan Garner and re-constructed adjoining Toad Hall, Goostrey in the 1970s.
Below: Church cottages with thatch in 1917.

Above: Church cottages with thatch removed in 1928.
Below: Church cottages in 1930, with the church and Red Lion to the right.

Above: Church Bank cottages. Three other thatched cottages were in this area in the 1890s. The furthest cottage was demolished and a house built set back from the road.
Below: Old Forge, Church Bank. Once an Inn and then a Smithy which closed in 1938

Above: Bridge Cottage and the entrance to the Bongs. Much altered (the roof was first thatched, then corrugated and now slate).
Below: Brookside Farm, Blackden Lane in 1971. Still has artificial "windows" painted on the brickwork to keep the symmetrical pattern. This was originally done to avoid paying window tax.

Above: a seat in the Bongs in 1925. Mr Lloyd Tunley, joiner, made the original seat.
Below: in 1999 a new seat was made, donated in memory
of Mr & Mrs Rimmington.

Above: Woodend farm, Winterbottom. From Church Bank the Bongs goes through to Mill Lane and Winterbottom (a half mile walk).
Below: Wood cottage, demolished 1994 and replaced with a new house.

FOUR VIEWS FROM CHURCH TOP

Right: looking north down Church Bank and Blackden Lane towards Blackden and Barnshaw.

Below: looking west down Main Road with Smallwoods general store on the left, the Crown Inn roof to the bottom right and the Manor House on the right.

Opposite top: looking south from Church Top in 1978 over the new village hall and school.

Opposite bottom: looking east towards the station. In the foreground is the Red Lion Inn and top centre is Cornbrook House (now The Grange).

Top: view of the Crown in 1913 with the farm buildings to the left and the house "Bank View" to the right.
Centre: Crown Inn Yard. George Massey stands in front of a decorated Rose Day cart with Jack, the waggoner, with the horse.
Bottom: the Crown Inn and farm buildings in 1950s.

INNS OF CHARACTER

Above: Crown Inn in 1888. This photo was taken soon after the name was changed from the Mainwaring Arms.

THE CROWN INN

THE OCCUPANCY OF the Crown Inn dates back to the 16th century. It is known that in the 17th century the property was two dwellings, part of which became a public house under the ownership of the Mainwaring family, hence the former title of 'The Mainwaring Arms'. This was run by the first known occupants, the Hobson family and it was known as a "free house" for years. In 1800, Peter Mee farmed the land and was landlord, then in 1851 Richard Knowles was victualler. The directory of Cheshire states that Benjamin Barber was the victualler of the "Mainwaring Arms" in 1860. The surrounding land became quite a large farm and the Mainwarings took over four cottages for farm workers, at what are now numbers 99, 101, 105 and 107 Main Road (now privately owned).

The name was changed to the 'Crown Inn and Farm' during the late 1800s, extra farm buildings having been built in 1835 surrounding the Inn (these buildings were demolished in 1966). In the December of 1965, Goostrey school children held their own Nativity Play in the old farm building, the play having been written by Goostrey's

Above: the Crown Inn in the 1930s.
Right: Cilla and Freda Worth of the Crown Inn circa 1930.
Below right: milkmaid at the Crown circa 1930.
Below: corn harvesting, Crown Fields.

famous children's book writer, Alan Garner, the title of which is "Holly from the Bongs". Smith's Brewery, owners at that time, made use of some of the land where the buildings had stood for extra car parking space. [Land beyond was sold for house building by Willans of Sale, in 1966 (now Brooklands Drive)]. The Edwards family were the next victuallers, followed by the Francis family. In the 1950s The Beech family had the Crown and farm, before moving on to the Belfry at Handforth. They took a special interest in catering and provided excellent restaurant facilities.

The Goodwin family were next to have the Crown selling Smith's ale then later Marston's. Sharpley's took over for a short period, then John and Margaret Lawton had the running of the establishment from 1961 to 1977, and very popular they were too. A warm welcome awaited, especially in winter, in more ways than one, for in the lounge would be the biggest, brightest coal fire (not approachable within feet!). John was always known as 'Cobby Lawton' since his days as a coal merchant in Holmes Chapel. In 1969, John had applied for a special licence to keep the public house open at night because of the influx of people in the district who were expected whilst the 'neighbours' at the Jodrell Bank Radio Telescope monitored the space landing on the moon. His was the only public house in the country open and John and Margaret had concocted a special Punch drink which included vodka (for the Russian involvement) and coke (for the Americans) giving it the title Moonglow. Sadly but not unexpectedly they ran out of all drink shortly after midnight.

Quite a number of alterations took place to the Crown during that period. Mr and Mrs Peter McGrath were the next popular tenants, building up a loyal following of customers with their good food and beer. In 1992, Marston's Brewery chose a number of public houses including the Crown for expansion, and to have a manager rather than a tenant. Gary Bridgewood and his wife Cynthia took over the management. The brewery added a new restaurant without destroying the character of the pub, which never closed during the refurbishment thanks to the landlord and lady, who are still at the Crown, and who make sure all regulars and visitors are most welcome *GR*

Below: the demolition of the Crown Inn farm buildings in 1966.

Above: harvesting at the Red Lion. Walter Knowles throws corn sheaves into the thresher and son Richard (left) bags up the corn.
Below: days of hunting outside the Red Lion in the 1980s.

Above: the Red Lion in 1895. To the left was the road that once ran down to Church Bank, coming out in front of the Forge cottage.

THE RED LION INN

THIS HOSTELRY WAS an inn, farm, general store, and on occasions a surgery. Built in the early C18th, it is said to have been occupied at least since 1711. A visiting dentist would also treat patients here. A tooth would be extracted without anaesthetic. Lydia Bagnall (later Smallwood), who lived in Goostrey all her life (93 years), remembered knocking at the door because of toothache in 1902, then running away in fear, only to be called back and persuaded to go in by the late Dr Lionel Picton's wife, who was assisting the dentist that day, and in no time at all the tooth was out! The Inn was first taken on by the Foden family and travellers from Macclesfield to Chester called here regularly in their horse-drawn vehicles. Then the Knowles family took over, Connie and Walter Knowles had two sons, Percy and Richard, very popular "mine hosts", although the Red Lion was very different in those days. The tap room had sawdust on the floor, a spittoon in the corner, always a roaring fire in the grate. It only had a six day licence, for serving beer only at one time. On Sundays refreshments and ale could only be served to visitors who had travelled to the village more than three miles. There was catering also on Rent Days.

The Red Lion, like the Crown Inn has been altered frequently this century. There have been many landlords including Jim Moran, Peter and Pat Magrath, David Hassall, Peter and Mary York and Frank Maguire. **GR**

Gooseberry Shows, 1924.

Goostrey Gooseberry Show held at the "Red Lion" Hotel, Goostrey, July 26th, 1924.

		Maiden Prize		Dwts.	Grs.
Hill	...		Lord Derby	15	1
Knowles	...	**Triplets**			
Tickle	...		Surprise	32	9
ea	...		Thatcher	28	6
	...		Fascination	27	6
Richardson	...	**Twins**			
Lennerley	...		Woodpecker		
Davies	...		Surprise	38	0
ea	...		Thatcher	36	1
Tickle	...		Leveller	34	13
ain	...		Surprise	34	10
bbins	...		Thatcher	33	9
Teal	...		Woodpecker	30	12
	...		Lord Derby	29	10
ain	...	**Steward's Prizes**		26	6
Davies	...		Ringer		
Richardson	...		Princess Royal	24	10
bbins	...		Woodpecker	24	3
ompson	...		Lord Derby	22	17
ldron	...		Woodpecker	22	7
			"	22	6
			"	21	0

1924 COMPETITION

Above: George Bayley, George Capper, Walter Knowles (Red Lion landlord) and John Henry Groves with their winning gooseberries.
Below left: Jim Whitehurst and his gooseberry pens.
Below centre: Walter Knowles displays a prize-winning gooseberry

Jodrell Bank Show, July 25.			Dwts.
J. Robinson	...(M.P.)...		Ringer
W. Robinson	...(Twins)...		London
J. Walton	...do...		London
I. Vaudry	...do...		Lord Derby
I. Street	...do...		Hit or Miss
W. Robinson	...(P.P.)...		London
J. Walton	...(S.P.)...		London
F. Wood	...do...		Leveller
I. Street	...do...		Hit or Miss
H. Birchall	...do...		Shiner
C. Parrott	...do...		Mount Pleasant
I. Vaudry	...do...		Lord Derby
J. Gallimore	...do...		Mount Pleasant
S. Warburton	...do...		London
P. Bailey	...do...		Leveller
I. Slater	...do...		Drill
F. Rathbone	...do...	Hero of the Nile
H. Gallimore	...do...	Hero of the Nile
F. Bentley	...do...		Leveller
L. Lewis	...do...		Leveller
J. Casey	...do...		Ringer
J. Barber	...do...		Antagonist
W. Davies	...do...		Companion
J. Gregory	...do...	Dan's Mistake
J. Walton	...RED...		London
J. Walton	...do...	Dan's Mistake
W. Robinson	...do...		Companion
J. Walton	...do...		Bobby
J. Walton	...do...		Lord Derby
J. Walton	...do...		Clayton
J. Walton	...do...		Falstaff
J. Walton	...do...		Viceroy
J. Walton	...YELLOW...		Leveller
I. Street	...do...		Hit or Miss
J. Robinson			Ringer

GOOSEBERRY GROWERS

Above: gooseberry growers quench their thirst at the Red Lion.

THE GOOSTREY GOOSEBERRY weigh-in and show was held here for many years. One resident, the late Ronald Fisher's father, had records dating back to the 1840s. In the 1880s, the gooseberry shows were held at Jodrell Hall. More recent records from 1896, show a marquee was erected at the rear of the Red Lion for the weigh-in and for the public to view later. The show continued annually even through the two world wars.

Rule books have to be adhered to, and very strict they are too. Even the transfer of bushes from one grower to another. Some of the first named varieties of gooseberry still win prizes, like Woodpecker, Lord Derby, Transparent etc. Closely guarded are the secrets of how they are fed, what you need in the soil to start a bed, how to ward off mildew, deal with too much sunshine, and deal with the wasps etc.

One tale of years ago; a young woman on-looker whispered to an older relative "D'you thinks they doctor them? The old woman champed her jaws slowly, tasting the air for truth and said (looking around her so's no-one was lip-reading, then with much discretion boomed) "Ah doan't know, but there's some daft beggars that sits out all day wi-em wi an umbrella o'er 'em – Barmy" said the old biddy.

Back in the 1920s Colin's [Smallwood] grandfather was guarding his plot the night

1999 COMPETITION
Top left: the gooseberries are displayed and ...
Top right: the judging begins ...
Centre left: the berries are weighed against
each other by Mr Lenehan and Mr Basford,
watched by Roy Hill and ...
Centre right: other anxious
entrants , and at last ...
Bottom right: Doug Carter is declared the
winner.

before picking was due, and at midnight his wife called him in for a cuppa. On his return to the plot, the prize gooseberries had all gone. Learning the procedure, I found that inspection of the plants was carried out by other members in intervals, and the evening before the show, members supervise each other's picking of berries, which are placed carefully in a box, on cotton wool, then the box is tied up and sealed with wax. The boxes, when taken to the show, are then inspected to make sure the seal has not been tampered with (the President having asked for this witnessing). Then the serious business is on, and growers are allowed to undo the boxes and look inside. A few anguished groans come from those whose would-be prize has burst in the box overnight.

Weighing begins in earnest, first with the Maiden Growers' berries (weighed against each other, until the heaviest is found), the weights being in Dwts (pennyweights) and grams. The twins are called for next; ie. two berries growing from the same stem (heartache for one new grower once when the wife separated them beforehand!) Triplets are next, then comes time for the weighing for the Premier Berry of the show. Then the best beaten berry is announced, down to the last one from each member. Next to be weighed are the coloured berries, plates of twelve of red, yellow, green and white (normal procedure is that a licensee attends with drinks as, one can understand, this is a thirsty, nail-biting business!). A special cup is presented to the winner of the best Premier Berry of all nine district shows in the Mid-Cheshire Gooseberry Association.

The 1999 Premier Berry was won by Goostrey's Doug Carter, weighing 36 pennyweights or seven grams. The Association Trophy was presented to Doug at a special dinner at the Crown Inn, when all other members of the Mid-Cheshire Show were invited. The trophy has other Goostrey growers' names on, in particular, Doug's father Frank, who won the trophy three years on the run. Frank was showing in 1942 and is still growing and showing in 1999 (57 years on)!

In 1961, there was trouble in "goosegogland" when the growers were banned from holding their show at the Red Lion after 65 or more years. The owner and landlord of the day, Mr Desmond Minikin, had changed the rules at the inn; he did away with the tap room where dominoes and darts were played, so the growers and fans had to move down to the Crown Inn. They hired a marquee for the lawn at the side of the Crown.

Now the event is held in the New Village Hall, on the last Saturday in July. **GR**

Above: (village postcard) Kennerleys shop was in the building on the right (now Kettles General Store).
Below: Margaret and George Kettle outside their store, decorated to celebrate 50 years of peace on VJ Day, 1995

A HISTORY OF GOOSTREY SHOPS

Above: Hurstfields grocers, circa 1900. Bread was made at the bakery to the left of the photo, 103 Main Road, until 1956. Between 1956 and 1975 it was delivered daily from Northwich.

ESSENTIAL SERVICES IN Goostrey during the 1800s and early 1900s were travelling salesmen; a tailor's shop, which was also a barber's; a school; a doctor who visited on horseback; a blacksmith, grocers, visiting dentist, tinker, butcher, baker, dressmakers, undertaker, two corn mills, and farms.

In 1888 to the early 1900s Mrs Partington had a small apartment set aside in the school house for selling her home made toffee (mainly for school children). In 1902, Plants had a bakery in the house where Mr & Mrs Kettle now have a General Shop (168 Main Road). Thompsons then had a bakers and grocery business there. After that Mr Sam Kennerley had a Post Office at the premises (on opening the door to enter, it set off the very loud clanging of a bell – situated above the door. The bell would still be making itself heard as their customers made their way out!). Other occupants, Mr & Mrs Reg Huddart, tried a greengrocery. This shop was then closed until Mr & Mrs Kettle took it over in 1960, as an electrical shop and also post office, later changing it to the General Store. What is now 105 Main Road, was Hurstfields grocers in the late

Above left: Kennerley's grocers shop in the 1900s with Samuel Kennerley Senior (known as the Boss). The premises are still used to sell groceries.
Above right: next door – the front of the present newsagents in the early 1900s, when it was still Carters the tailors.

Right: the milk sledge in 1942 outside the paper shop.

Above: Hurstfields grocers, 1959. The grocers closed in 1975 and is now a private house (105 Main Road).

1890s. At the rear, the building of what is now 103 became a bakery, baking their own bread until 1956. The grocers shop closed in 1975.

Number 182 Main Road was originally Kennerleys Grocers Shop in the 1880s, which changed hands quite a number of times, Beswicks, Turtons, Crombleholmes etc and in 1999 Derek & Amanda Burgess took over (along with the post office business which has moved at least six times to four different houses within 50 yards of one another over the last 50 years). Derek and Amanda have also taken on the "off licence" business.

The newsagents was originally Sam Carter's tailors shop (late 1800s), the family owning the premises until the 1970s, as the post office and newspaper shop. In the 1930s and 1940s the tailor had the rear of premises as a barbers and would cut men's and boys' hair at a cost of 3d. During 1939/45 war it was the ARP post. Since the 1970s there have been quite a number of owners, Gibsons, Jones, Hughes, Jeffs, Mr, Mrs & Matthew Nield, and now Mr Razi. Fred and Lydia Smallwood started a boot and shoe repair and cycle shop in two sheds on the front of Rose cottage, plus the shoe and cycle business which Fred had at the rear. In 1932 they moved to 216 Main Road. This general store was kept up by Lydia from 1950 until taking an early retirement at the age of 89! The shop was sold to the Ollertons, who opened up as a 'sporting lines' shop,

Above: Lydia Smallwood outside their first shop plus repair shed in the 1920s (also right). The buildings of the Crown Inn are in the background.
Below: The Trading Post, Booth Bed Lane.

Above: the Smallwood's later general store before footpaths. This building is now a private residence (216 Main Road).

selling fishing tackle, guns, etc for three years. Jack Darlington had a small butchers shop where Bodimedes (Cheshire House) is now, until 1955. It then became an electrical shop (Briscolls) until 1972, when it was demolished to become known as Cheshire House.

There was also a butchers, run by Mr Davies, at 99 Main Road in the 1890s and then he started a cobblers shop on the premises, in what had been a horse-drawn tram. In the 1930s, Mr Hollinshead had a small wooden shop at the side of Morgans house (142 Main Road) selling sweets and tobacco.

The ladies Sumner and Scott started a small grocers shop between New Platt Lane and Main Road (1), Miss Polly Wilkinson joining the ladies. Then the business was acquired by Mr Francis Smallwood, who extended the shop. Eventually it was sold to Seymour Meads, the grocers, who also had an off-licence. Then Mr Tony Barnsley bought the premises and had a DIY store. He4 converted it back into a private house in 1988/9.

In the 1960s, a new shop was built at Booth Bed Lane for Malcolm Wright, selling grocery and greengrocery called The Trading Post. This was taken over by Lance Gibson and then the present owners, the O'Donaghue's. A small shop opened up adjoining, changing frequently from hairdressers – greengrocers – clothes shop etc.

Bonner Law had an upholstery business where the precinct is now. This was part of the property known as Tinker Tomkinsons. He mended pots and pans. After he died,

Above: Tinker Tomkinson's cottage following a fire in 1909.
Below: In 1973 the precinct of four shops was built on this site (opposite the Acreage).

Above: Tinker Tomkinson's cottage in 1907. Tinker mended pots and pans for the villagers.

the old thatched cottage burnt down. Four new shops were built on this site in 1973. Initially, as Hughs, estate agents; John Davids, hairdressers; Denier Modes, dress shop and Ian Ibbottsons, butchers. When the dress shop closed Mr Ibbottson bought it and extended his butchers shop. It was resold in 1992 when it became a children's wear shop. The estate agents became an "off-licence" but has since closed down. Other changes of ownership have taken place.

Misses Shingler & Johnson were the village dressmakers from the 1920s to 1940s. teaching other young ladies their skills.

A number of travelling salesmen regularly called on the villagers. The fire station was situated at the side of Morgans during the 1939/45 war. Mr Morgan's garage was family run, carrying out repairs and the petrol pumps kept busy until a few years ago. There was also petrol to be had at the front of Bates (60 Main Road). These premises were known as Mount Pleasant Farm and Mr & Mrs Bates then opened the West End Café, which became a haven for cyclists, and many have wonderful memories of the hospitality received there. Indeed, in 1949 Mrs Bates acquired a coveted medal from the Manchester & District Cycling Association and became the first President of the Ladies Section, a post she held for seven years. The girls presented her with a Gold Medal to mark their appreciation. A war-time soldier recalled surprising his officer (having been to Bates Café many times as a cyclist) remarking, "I know a good place

Above: the indefatigable Mrs Bates with one of her renowned home-made Christmas puddings – *Mrs Super Cook* and she loved every minute of it!
Right: top to bottom early days at the café to the finished property, complete with petrol pumps.
Below: end of the road – demolition of the café in 1999.

Above: a meal at Bates café for ex-servicemen circa 1945.

for a cuppa! quite near here". He was told to direct the two trucks, and getting out at Bates's, being recognised as one of her old cyclists, they were all provided with poached eggs on toast and tea. Mrs Bates would not take a penny, 'too pleased to do something for our brave boys'. Mr and Mrs Bates started a caravan park. Later they had help from their son Peter and daughter Rene, developing a park of high standard, in a lovely rural setting, which became part of the community life in Goostrey. New standards of comfort, new structures befitting technology and with all the modern convenience has changed "Batesville" as it was known, into a haven for residents. After Mrs Bates's death, Rene helped her father. Later she and her husband were to run the establishment, finally closing the café and then retiring for health reasons. The café was well used locally over all the years, for wedding celebrations, functions of every description, regular meetings, for British Legion, Over 60s, etc. In 1999, the actual café was knocked down and the site used to rebuild for private use.

Mr W Whittick operated the first taxi service, from Bridge House in the mid 1930 period. Challinor & Sons have been joiners in the village, first wheelwrights and making hen cotes, hay sheds etc in the early 1920s, and now dutch barns and portable buildings in timber and steel.

Luke Brothers set up a flourishing market gardeners at the rear of the newspaper and grocers shops, selling mainly tomatoes and chrysanthemums, both wholesale and retail. When they moved out of the village the land was sold for building, becoming "The Acreage". *GR*

Above: Victor Holden, traveller in ironmongery and paraffin.
Below: Morgan's garage and petrol station.

Above: Morgan's heavy breakdown truck.
Below: boys wait in Dave Rees's car, 1960.

Above left: District Bank 1892. These premises were once used as a village school.
Above right: District Bank 1940, went on to become the National Westminster Bank.
Below: the National Westminster Bank in 1990 just before it closed.

Above: Wayside grocers, No. 1 Main Road. Originally Sumner Scott & Wilkinson, then F & J Smallwood and later Seymour Meads.
Below: Wayside stores later became Barnsley's Hardware and DIY but has now been converted back into a private home.

Above: station staff 1891. Two signalmen, clerk, and two porters with the station master Mr Locket (centre). There are no staff at all today.
Below: Manchester to Crewe train pulling into Goostrey station.

GOOSTREY (March 24th, 1951)
The Manchester to Crewe stopping train, with 'Crab'
42887 in charge, pulls into Goostrey Station.

GOOSTREY STATION

Above: station houses built for the staff in the 1890s.

IN 1841 THE construction of the Manchester to Crewe railway lines was completed at Goostrey. Keystones placed in the centre of the road bridge commemorated this, bearing the engineer's name G W Buck and the date 1841 above it. The stones were removed when the line was electrified.

In 1891 the first passenger train stopped at Goostrey station, for people to journey to Manchester. The line to Crewe was also made available for passengers and goods. In the 1890s and the first quarter of the 1900s, willow was cut from Goostrey willow beds and sent by train to Manchester for basket making.

Also at that time, London received approximately 100 million gallons of milk per year by rail transport. Collections from stations, including Goostrey, were made in the late evenings, for delivery in London next day. The milk was transported in large churns. Later in the 1930s village boys would collect and take trucks loaded with eggs to the station, from Mill House Farm, Summerfields, The Beeches, Primrose Cottage etc to load on the trains to be taken to Sandbach, Stockport and Chelford markets.

Above: porter Jim Street on the platform in 1956.
Below: first electric train on a trial run in 1960.

Above: a fond farewell at Goostrey station after a village wedding, 1930.

Below: One very foggy afternoon in late 1937 this autogiro landed near Goostrey station. Sid Grindy was paid 7s.6d to act as night watchman over the aircraft.

National Schools, Goostrey 1896,
Head Master; Mr. Duckworth

Above: pupils and staff in 1896. Top left is headmaster for 42 years Mr Robert Duckworth. Second from right on the top row is teacher Miss Knowles, and far right is Margaret Duckworth, daughter of Robert who later became a teacher herself.
Below: another class from the 1890s with headmaster Robert Duckworth on the left. Bottom right is Mrs Partington of School House, who made and sold treacle toffee and humbugs to the children.

GOOSTREY SCHOOL

Above: the village school circa 1905.

THE EARLIEST REFERENCES to a school, were made in Church records, when in 1640 there was a school mentioned. Mr Howlt was in charge of the school located in the churchyard (1640-1645). As in most country parishes the school was near the church where the curate or parson gave instructions to the local children.

Mr Z Crofton was the next curate and Master from 1645-1648. Mr Newcome took over from 1648-1653. In 1648 the school needed repairs and 8d was paid to a carpenter to repair the school house for Mr Newcome. In 1666 there are references to disputes about the school and £1 2s 6d was paid to Mr Samuel Smallwood for drawing "An arbitracon Bond, two grants on parchment to settlinge of ye schoole" (the old school building was clearly attached to the church).

In 1667 the school was at The Bankes, next to the Forge. This building was pulled down in 1703 (Mr Matthew Holford teacher at that time). In 1685 the late Elizabeth Haselhurst endowed the school with £200 for a Free School. This is recorded on her flagstone in the church yard. In 1775 a reference is made that a school was built with two rooms over it for masters.

Mr John Pass was headmaster at that time, from 1770 to 1810. In 1812 yet another

Above: a 1909 class.
Below: Goostrey school in the later 1930s.

school was built, this time on the site where the District Bank/National Westminster Bank was (now 93 Main Road) at a cost of £90. Mr Johnathan Harding was Head and Parish Clerk from 1810 to 1856. Mr Pass and Mr Hardy are buried side by side near the West tower of Goostrey Church. In 1856 the school on Main Road next to the School House was built for £689 on land given by Mr Henry Mainwaring Esq.

Mr Charles Goostrey was the first master at the new school and Miss Sarah Harding was mistress. Mr Thomas Baskerville, Mr Rideout and Mr Winstanley were masters for a short period – then came Mr Robert Duckworth from 1872 to 1914. There are still a few who remember being taught by Mr Duckworth (an article has already been written about him by the Smallwoods and is available on request). During that period there are details of successful whist drives etc. in 1911 and an adverse report of a Government Inspector demanding that certain improvements be carried out at the school.

It was not desirable to hand over the Church School to the County Council, putting it on the rates, therefore a garden party and other means of raising the necessary money for repairs had to be considered. The school managers had a considerable sum of money in hand – about £60, and Mr Egerton-Leigh kindly granted that a garden party be held at Jodrell Hall to raise the rest of the money needed. £130 was raised for surfacing of the playground, new cloakroom etc.

On Mr Duckworth's death, Miss Annie F Lees, an emergency teacher took over until Mr J Holland was appointed. Mr Holland taught for two years and then was called up for military service. Mr Oulton from the staff of Davenham C of E School took over as head teacher until Mr Holland returned in 1918. In 1919 Mr Holland took up a headmastership at Furnace Vale.

Miss Marion Marlor completed her two year course at Crewe Training College and was appointed as Assistant Certified Teacher in the school. Mr Charles Barlow was headmaster from 1919 to 1948.

Colin Smallwood recalls some of the things that took place when Mr Barlow was headmaster:– Battery hens were a feature during the 1920-38 period, when poultry owners were encouraged to allow pupils to bring them to school. A poultry house was situated within the headmaster's garden for about twelve birds. Eggs were collected by scholars and these were weighed and registered, then sold. The money from the eggs paid expenses for the corn etc needed for feeding. A daily supply of milk was delivered to the school, each scholar having a third of a pint bottle at the 11am break. During the cold winter months, some of the milk would be boiled before serving in a cup or mug, but hot milk topped with skin was not a favourite with some pupils. Canning of fruit, such as gooseberries and damsons was performed successfully under the head's tuition (the fruit being in perfect condition when opened, several months later). Also book-binding of magazines was undertaken in the senior boys' class. A very sharp knife

Above left: headmaster Charles Barlow encouraged children to rear poultry.
Above right: Charles Barlow and his family.
Centre right: the school in the 1950s, in front of which are the remains of the school's war-time shelter.
Below: Mrs Illgmann with her school band, 1958/9.

and steel rule made a smooth edge to each volume but eventually a modern and improved cutting tool made a much better finish. Mr Barlow participated in all aspects of village life, especially where the school or scholars could be involved.

Assisted by his eldest son Edwin, numerous school concerts, songs, sketches, monologues etc. were held in the Village Hall. The profits from these concerts were used to buy a film projector. Films from the library were shown occasionally and in 1937 a film entitled *The Gap* depicted what was supposed to be an air-raid over the south coast of England and on to the capital, London. News and nature films were the usual programme.

During the 1930s, there a very good "rotating" library at the school and every few weeks books were exchanged, being sent back via the local railway station (boys wheeling the books up to the station in a cart and collecting the replacements). For the senior scholars who could swim, Friday afternoons were eagerly awaited, when Cooks coach from Sandbach would convey them to Saltersford School (Holmes Chapel) swimming pool for a period of one hour. Those who could not swim were allowed to splash about but, alas, no instructors or lifeguards were available!

A Parents' Day was held in the school in July 1923. Written invitations were sent out and some 40 parents availed themselves of the method of instruction employed in the school, which they probably found very different from what was customary in their own school days. In the infants room, children gave demonstrations in singing, recitations and games, while in the large rooms specimens of the children's work, writing and arithmetic were exhibited, showing the steady progress over a number of years. Mr Barlow explained the advantages derived from newer methods of instruction, congratulating the children on improved discipline, as evident by the fewer entries in the Punishment Book.

In that period, Attendance Officers from the school board would visit the homes of children to see why they had not been attending and on more than one occasion, the children were escorted to school if they had no good reason for being away. School extensions were made in 1958 and 1967, a new hall being built plus a kitchen, washrooms, toilets and also two classrooms with toilets on the first floor.

In the 1960s the school became overcrowded because of many new houses being built in the village, after sewage pipes were installed through the village, but thankfully doing away with the old soil toilets (and boys taking nettles round the back of the old toilets and trying to sting the girls' bottoms!).

Before the new building was completed, two mobile classrooms were erected in the school yard, then a third, after which Goostrey Methodist Chapel Sunday School room was used for a class in 1962, also a class was held in the (old) village hall. Meanwhile the new school for reception to seven year olds was built alongside a new Village Hall in 1977. **GR**

Rules of the School

Parents who wish to enter their children at the school, may do so by applying to the Master on any Monday morning at 9 o'clock or to the incumbent of Goostrey at the Parsonage. Parents are requested to pay particular attention to the following rules:-

1. The children are to assemble at the school on every weekday at 9o'clock and every afternoon at half past 1o'clock except Saturday which is a holiday.

2. The school hours are from 9 till 12 and half past 1 till 4 pm

3. The children must be sent to school neat in person and dress.

4. No child may stay away from school without leave from the master or mistress or from the manager.

5. Leave of absence will be readily granted, either by application personally or by note, this application must be made before, and not after, the child absents itself.

6. If any child come late, or absent (without leave) a ticket will be sent requiring a reason from the parent.

7. If the ticket be disregarded the child will not be allowed to attend the school until a satisfactory answer has been given by the parent.

8. The school fees are as follows:- quarterly 7s, 5s, 3s weekly 3d and 2d to be paid in advance. If there are three children from 1 family attending, a reduction will be made.

9. There will be holidays at Easter, Midsummer and Christmas.

WILLIAM E DICKSON MA Goostrey 24th 1858

An NB at the bottom of the school rules read as follows:

Parents are earnestly requested to carry on the school work at home by reminding their children that to "Fear God and to keep his commandments is the whole duty of man".

PERSONAL MEMORIES

GOOSTREY IN THE 1920-1930s
by Arthur Jarvis

GOOSTREY SCHOOL. I remember Mr Barlow, the headmaster. Also pupils like Albert Groves, Dim Hamilton, Gwen Jones, the Sweatmans, Smallwoods, Hurstfields, John Simpson and a host of others. Every lad in those days carried a catapult and was often in trouble for shooting at pigeons that rested in the school roof. I well remember Charlie Barlow dishing out six of the best when he caught as at it. Also the sand martins in the sand hole opposite the Red Lion. We used to put our finger in the hole where they nested and they would peck quite sharply.

The Crown in those days had only a six day licence and closed on Sundays, but I well remember on Sunday seeing some Irishmen drunk in the back yard and Dick Worth, the landlord, trying to get them into a loose box. Of course the Red Lion had its characters as well. With Jack Groves a regular attending both daytime and evening and he always drank his beer out of a pot mug and not a regular glass. Walter Knowles the landlord always wore a bowler hat both working outside and when he was serving out of a jug and of course, Constance his wife came in for a bit of ribbing as well. There were village characters like Putty Carter, who lived at the top of Putty Alley (Bank View). He kept pedigree pigs for breeding, then used to take them round the farms in a horse and float. Also in Putty Alley lived the Platts, Freddie and Harold. I remember Harold shooting his eye out with his catapult. He is now buried in Stratford-upon-Avon, near my brother Frank.

I remember an old roadman named Riley Rider and one night going home from school John Hamner and myself took his old tricycle and rode down the hill towards Shear Brook, but John couldn't turn the corner so we finished up in the hedge.

At Hurstfields bakehouse we used to gather to watch them pulling loaves out of the ovens and Fred Smallwood at his shop across the road would call out his famous "Howya" whenever anyone passed that he knew.

One thing that has died out now was the running of milk churns to the station, to catch the milk train about 7 am. There was a man named Ryder who lived down past the Mill near the bongs who had a very fast horse and he used to race other men. It was a wonder there was never an accident.

May Day or Rose Day was the outstanding event in the village in the old days. I can recall Mrs Bayley coming to school to select the children for various roles and the best thing I remember was the Maypole plaiting, and if you were one of those you were somebody. One of the great delights of course was the Brass Band that led the procession, it fairly made you march along.

Another event which was prominent in those days was Armistice Sunday service at the War Memorial. The Boys Reform School Band from Holmes Chapel always led by Captain Dronsfield, of Blackden Manor. I also remember going to Chapel Sunday School and seeing Boss Kennerley, who was an imposing figure with a very loud voice. He also ran a grocery round and his pies and sausages were that hot with pepper they blistered your mouth but at 2d each the pies were worth it! **GR**

Above: Goostrey scouts waiting on and serving refreshments to footpath group walkers (see page 139). A Goostrey Walk and Strolls booklet is available at local shops.

PERSONAL MEMORIES

GOOSTREY COMMUNITY PRIMARY SCHOOL , NOVEMBER 1999
Mrs Valerie Edwards (January 1983 to present day)

WHEN I WAS appointed head teacher on 1st January 1983, my first observation was that I was the first woman to be head (job description – Head Teacher not Head Mistress!) and my second was that this school was very special, as the average length of service for each head teacher this century was 22 years.

Although many things have changed since that first day in 1983 (notably our name), many things have remained the same – the two buildings, the playgrounds, the children (different but the same!) and some members of staff. We still have strong links with the church and local community and we still fund raise in much the same way. However it's what goes on inside the building that has really changed. Children are no longer "seen but not heard". On the contrary, they have rights under the law. However, alongside rights they have to be taught responsibility. Parents have a great deal of power in helping to shape the future of education. They serve on the governing body, which, corporately is responsible for decision-making in the school, financially as well as for the curriculum. Primary education is now very prescriptive, becoming more like secondary education as we know it. We no longer teach reading, writing and arithmetic, with the occasional art, music and PE lesson thrown in when it's convenient and on a sunny day drop everything and go for a walk in the Bongs. Now, from the age of four to eleven, all children in England and Wales are taught the same National Curriculum - English, Mathematics, Science, Information Technology, Design and Technology, History, Geography, Art, Music, Physical Education, Religious Education and Personal and Social Development. No time to stand and stare.

It isn't all doom and gloom. Bullying by either children or adults is no longer swept under the carpet but discussed and solved by teaching strategies for coping with it, in the same way as for any problem in the curriculum. Premises are bright and cheerful, enhanced by children's art work which is one outcome of their study work. We approach the millennium with a new Multimedia Suite, opened by our Member of Parliament, Mrs Ann Winterton. This comprises five new linked computers (in addition to the ones in the classrooms) a scanner, one colour and one black and white printer, a listening centre, a television, a digital camera, a study area and last but not least, an up to date library of BOOKS! The old alongside the new technology and equally valued.

Goostrey School's new name "Community" best describes its place in the local community. It belongs to the village, nurturing and encouraging our young people to grow in every sense of the word. I am proud to be a part of it - long may it flourish. **GR**

GOOSTREY MAY FESTIVAL 1901

Above: the 1901 Goostrey May Day Festival photo

A most enjoyable festival was held in a field kindly lent by Mr Worth, when the children assembled at the school in their gay and gorgeous dresses, headed by a band, had a procession through the village, the honour of being May Queen is gained by regular attendance at school, and this year Mary Worth was the fortunate young lady. Very pretty in white satin frock with a train lined with blue and trimmed with swans down, her little Majesty was attended by four maids of honour, Louie Evans, Emilie Cumberbirch, Mildred Peak and Maggie Worth. They were attired in white and each carried a bouquet of flowers. The remainder of the characters are as follows:- Britannia, Annie Ward; Fairy, Mary Stanley; Bo-Peep, Minnie Moss; Cinderella, Rosa Woodcock; Chinese Lady and Gent, Ethel Egerton and Walter Hurstfield; Mary and little lamb, Francis Woodcock; Little boy blue, Willie Carter; Spring, Esther Webb; Summer, Annie Hocknell; Autumn, Frances Smallwood; Winter, Edith Cash; Buttercups, Mary Tickle; Daisies, Annie Davis; Violets, Bertha Mann; Jack and Jill, Harry Gibbons and Mary Goodier; Nurse, Jeannie Parrott; Doctor, Fred Plumb; Butcher Phillip Newton; Baker, Arthur Ward; Policeman, Arthur Cumberbirch; Milk Maids, Ada Ward and Margaret Warburton; John Bull, Sidney Glover; Crown Bearer, Percy Plant; Sceptre, George Cash; Sword, George Hamilton; Tom Thumb and Wife, Arthur Wood and May Warburton; Soldiers, Frank Johnson, John Basford, Harold Cash and Harry Egerton; Bugler, Richard Lee; Soldiers on Horseback, John Knowles, Sidney Platt and Richard Worth; Flower girls, Lizzie Dakin, Winifred Holland, Lucy Warburton, Jessie Dale, Sarah Egerton, Olive Newton and Winnie Clarke; Sailor Boys, Tom Wardleworth, Walter and Fred Holland, John Wood and Harry Clarke; Highlanders, Alfred Locket, Albert Groves, Ernest Plant, Augustus Goodman, Bertie and Harry Hardy, Ethel Thomson, Alice Bell, Ada Hamilton, Nora Bell, Maggie Woodcock and Mary Shingler; Tambourine Girls and Maypole, Dorothy and May Goodman, Nora Plant, Louie Bell, Gladys Evans, May Jervis, Edith Peake, Rachel Bell, Edith Tickle, Bertha Thomson and Edith Hamilton. Plaiting at the Maypole was done in a marvellously accurate manner, after a circuit round the village and the crowning and other dancing. Tea followed in the school-room. Committee members were Mrs Clarke, Mrs Dale, Mr Plumb. Children were trained by Misses Glazebrook, Knowles and Hocknell. Valuable assistance was given by Mrs Lockett, Mrs Brandreth and Misses Daniels and E Duckworth.
Wilmslow Advertiser, 1901

GOOSTREY ROSE FESTIVAL

Above: 1907 Rose Queen – Miss Marion Marlor makes her way to the field.
The house on the right is Bank View, without the village hall to its side.

THE FESTIVAL BEGAN in 1907, with a brief change of pattern during the World War years. The first queen was Miss Marion Marlor, her friends Emily Cumberbirch and Margaret Worth helping with the arrangements, financing themselves and ending the day with a grand profit of 2d which they shared! Emily was the next queen. A Bible signed by the President of the year was, and still is, given to the queen. Much work goes on in the village prior to the event. Early in the year a party is given for all children who took part the previous year, then the new queen is elected, along with two ladies-in-waiting. This selection was first made by the children, then by the committee, and afterwards by independent judges from outside the area. The village children meet to decide which characters they will be. Some original costumes are still used, the majority made by the villagers.

With very few exceptions the festival, has been held on the last Saturday in June, with a parade through the village. The Queen elect performs her first duty by placing a wreath at the cenotaph. The procession, consisting of the retiring Queen, various decorated floats, farm carts and cars filled with children and adults, Morris dance

Above: 1907 Festival: hoop-la stalls in days when hats were a must.
Below: Saltersford school band playing for the 1928 Festival.

troupes, one or two bands, occasionally the Cheshire Dairy Queen and other queens from the surrounding area, then makes its way to the field. A throne awaits the Queen and John Bull has the task of taking the various groups up to the throne and announcing them. He also has the task of crowning the new Queen. During the late 1990s a dance has followed in the evening in the new village hall.

Reference has already been made to the fact that the festival was started 25 years ago, but the story of how it came into being is interesting as an illustration of the lasting influence which the simple action of children can effect. The idea of a Rose Queen Festival originated with Miss Cumberbirch and her school friend Miss Worth, who though quite young at the time had very definite ideas as to how such an event should be run. In the first place they realised that funds were essential and so they first tackled the financial aspect of the question by obtaining subscriptions. The businesslike way in which they went about the matter impressed others and so a definite organisation came into being, and the festival was established on a firm basis. It was a graceful act on the part of the committee to ask Miss Cumberbirch, whose brother is now secretary, to take a definite part in the twenty-fifth anniversary festival. **GR**

Below: dog-cart and Shetland pony with (top left) the old air-raid shelter at the school, 1950s.

Above: Edward and Robert Simpson of Dromedary Lodge take part in the Festival on board their father's float.
Below: Piccaninnies line the route of the flower girls and other characters.

Above: Rose Day dancers with the Crown buildings in the background.
Below: May Pole dancing is part of the Festival each year.

Above: Year 2000 Rose Queen elect.
Below: Rose Day spectators, 1956.

GOOSTREY ROSE FESTIVAL JUNE 6th 1914
Statement of Accounts

RECEIPTS

		£.	S.	D.	£.	S.	D.
At Gate:	R Dakin		8	6			
	A Cumberbirch	2	8	9			
	W Lambert	1	15	6			
	T Hamner	2	18	0			
	J Basford	2	8	9			
					9	19	6
Ring:						17	0
Teas:	W Lambert	2	5	0			
	J Basford	2	13	6			
	J Dakin		1	0			
	S Hamner	2	6	0			
	Mrs C Dakin		1	0			
					7	6	6
Dancing:	J Basford	1	12	0			
	A Cumberbirch		8	6			
	R Dakin	2	18	6			
	Jas. Dakin		5	6			
					5	4	6
Ice Cream Men:						6	0
Donkeys:						5	0
Collecting Boxes:		1	10	6			
	less prize money		14	0			
						16	6
Coconuts:					1	13	8
Houpla (for Dolly stall):					8	8	3
Fortune Tellers:					1	1	6
Sale of Cakes etc.:						1	4
					£35	19	9

EXPENDITURE

		£.	S.	D.	£.	S.	D.
Band:					4	15	0
Tents & Tables:					5	8	0
Dancing Troupes:	Plant Girls		10	0			
	Goostrey Mixtures	1	1	0			
	Grecian Festival	3	5	0			
	Falcon Pageant	2	15	0			
					7	11	0
Police:						6	10
Hire of Costumes:						10	0
Printing:						8	6
Art Muslin for Maypole:					2	11	0
Coconuts:	Balls		1	4			
	Nuts	1	1	0			
	Carriage			10			
					1	3	2
Bible:			5	0			
Ticket Rolls:				1	0		
Confectionery:	Hurstfield	1	16	3			
	Kennerley	1	8	0			
	Plant	2	5	3			
	Pritchard	1	10	9			
	Cutters Up		4	0			
					7	4	3
Childrens Sports:						6	0
Lurries						10	0
Band Allowance:						8	7
Carriage on Costumes:						1	0
T Rufus exps. tips etc.						2	4
Fortune Tellers Costumes:						5	0
Dyer:						2	6
Marlor, labour etc:					1	8	0
Houpla:					2	11	3
Pickstock (clearing tent etc):						1	6
Advertising:						7	6
Guardian:					1	3	0
Mrs Worth milk:						2	6
Carriage on box to Denton:							6
Postage & Stationery:					5	8	
Balance						8	9
					£35	19	9

The Accounts were signed T. Rufus (Hon. Sec.)

In October 1918 the Military Cross was awarded posthumously to Captain Thomas Rufus for devotion to duty and a particularly gallant act. His Company was very heavily attacked and he rallied his men with great coolness and a total disregard to danger – "He won his distinction many times over".

Above: 1908 Morris dance troupe.
Below: Morris dance troupe from the 1950s including, front, Harold Maddock, leader.

THE MORRIS DANCERS OF GOOSTREY

Above: 1905. The first Morris dance troupe with the Crown Inn in the background. centre is Mr Chapman and Mr Marlor is to the right. Thomas and Walter Hurstfield were two of the troupe pictured.

THE FIRST MORRIS team was all male and began in 1907, when Goostrey had its own troupe of dancers. Mrs Elsie Maddock re-formed a troupe in the village after the 1939/45 war, in time for Goostrey Rose Day. There were eight lads and eight lassies, the men wore grey trousers and white shirts and the girls, grey skirts and white blouses and they danced quite well. An adjudicator happened to see them and said to Elsie, "I am putting your troupe down for dancing at Davenham show next year" and he confirmed later that he had done so. The problem was mainly financial – they needed an acceptable outfit so, after discussions, they borrowed £8 from the Rose Festival Committee. Then Elsie and Mabel Lester took themselves off to Stockport market, looked around and spotted some striped material (Elsie fell for the blue and white) so they purchased enough to make eight skirts and eight ties and sashes for the men.

The next problem was the men's trousers and they wanted white ones and after many problems they managed to borrow enough. They persuaded Ida Carter of the paper shop to let them have packs of white crepe paper for a"special offer" price, then all sixteen met at Elsie's house, with instructions to bring pieces of wood, six inches in length - like brush handles, so that they could cut the crepe paper and fasten them together for the shakers (two each) which they were to carry. One member had cut two lengths off a farm rake, another had cut a broom handle up (Elsie and Harold getting the blame for their deeds!). They finally got a presentable outfit, then improved a tin trunk by painting it white with blue stripes and the letters Goostrey MD on, to take the costumes around in. They ordered the biggest coach they could– a 26 seater – to take themselves and supporters to Davenham. Many supporters had turned up, so they got two forms out of Goostrey Village Hall and put them down the centre of the bus, then straddled the forms and went, packed almost beyond capacity, to Davenham (would have been illegal today).

Elsie, who was not dancing, thought they had danced quite well. Needless to say they were thrilled and delighted when they were declared the winning morris dance troupe. They still have the trophy and many others. Elsie organised the troupe for over 20 years and went on to be a national judge. The morris dancers of Goostrey and various other troupes, competed at Goostrey Rose Days for many years. It was usual to have around twelve troupes competing from Manchester, Liverpool, Wigan, Warrington, Moulton etc. – coming to Goostrey was a highlight for them. They would have soup at the Crown Inn and compete for the prizes on the Rose Festival field. **GR**

Below: Morris dance troupe from the 1950s including, far right, Elsie Maddock, organiser and now Morris Dance judge.

GOOSTREY: PEOPLE AND GROUPS

Top: 1939-45 Goostrey Home Guard, whose HQ was the "Shooting Box".
Centre: Savannah band 1928.
Bottom: a presentation to Mr Harrison. Left to right councillors J Bailey, B Rodgers, D Harrison, J Lawton, F Lloyd, J Barber (chairman), A T Rees, G Hulme and L Grimsditch.

Top left: Egerton Leigh family of Jodrell Hall.
Top right: chimney sweep.
Centre and bottom left: Goostrey boy scouts camping in the Bongs, 1930.
Right: John Lawton, Crown Inn landlord 1961-77.

Above: scabious pickers in the snow at Barnshaw Hall.
Below: the Main Road under snow, 1970.

Below: clearing snow at Booth Bed in 1940.

Above: Armistice Parade in the cemetery, 1950s.
Below: Armistice parade through the village in the 1990s.

Above: Second World war firemen.

Above: Cheshire special constables with, third from left on middle row, Thomas Hurstfield.
Below: early days of Goostrey Women's British Legion, marching past
the dais and flag on the Bog Bean.

Above: ceremonial duties of Rose Queen Hazel Challinor.
Below: British Legion parade from the 1980s.

Above: Goostrey children on a nature walk.
Below: The first concert for 5-year-olds to a watching audience of parents, 1985.

Above: 1960s Farmers Ball.
Below: Over 60s meal with helpers at Bates Café.

Above: Goostrey traction engine enthusiast Jimmy Dakin, who re-built this ("Winnie") and other engines.
Below: John and Geoffrey Challinor with one of their engines at the 1967 Astle Park rally. In 1963 £802 was raised for the Goostrey Playing Fields Association.

Above left: 1964 tree planting ceremony. **Above right:** Mr and Mrs Groves.
Below left: school childrenon nature study.
Below right: ladies and the Royal Mail – M/s Stockton, Lloyd and Dakin.

Below left: early computer lessons, Goostrey Primary School, 1992
Below right: Jimmy Edwards at the Crown Inn.

Above: members of the Goostrey Painting Group display their Millennium Calendar art.
Below: Goostrey's Wine and Beer Making Society.

Above: WI v. Goostrey Men cricket match, 1975. The men were challenged again in 2000 for the Millennium game.
Below left: in 1973 the WI presented a village sign, placed on the Bog Bean. Mrs Peggy Jones (President) and Mr James Schofield (Parish Council Chairman) are on the right.
Below right: Goostrey Flower Club show.

GOOSTREY WOMEN'S INSTITUTE

Above: WI Anniversary meal, provided in the old village hall by Mrs Bates and helpers.

By the present secretary, Mrs Norah Relph

GOOSTREY WI WAS formed in November 1921 and since then has been a part of village life. It has always been aware of national matters and indeed put forward resolutions for consideration from time to time and kept up to date, celebrating anniversaries, competing in the Cheshire Shows and holding its own biannual show etc. The membership card in those early days stated:

National Federation of Women's Institutes MEMBERSHIP CARD

Goostrey Women's Institute 23rd November 1921

For Home and Country EXCISE REVENUE 1d one penny 1d

"To unite in promoting any work which makes for the betterment of our home and advancement of our people and the good of our country"

Meetings are held on the third Wednesday of each month in Goostrey Village Hall, originally in afternoons, but in the evenings at 7.30 pm now. Each meeting consists of a business session, an outside speaker, refreshments and social time for games and quizzes. Each month there is a competition for members to enter, connected in some way with the speaker's subject. Meetings open with the members singing *Jerusalem* and end with the *National Anthem*.

Above: WI – painting on china. **Below:** planting daffodils for the village.

Mrs Lionel Picton of Holmes Chapel was the first speaker, on "The feeding of babies, clothing for children and about food and recreation for adults". 63 members were present. The January meeting of 1922 records that owing to prevalence of influenza and the very bad state of the roads from snow and frost, only 32 members were present. The new small room at the hut (now youth centre) was used for the first time. Dr Lionel Picton was the speaker at the 6th meeting, arriving at 3.45 pm. He gave a most interesting address, dealing with "Cuts, Burns and Scalds", also a few hints on the care of the teeth and how to breathe properly through the nose. He illustrated his meaning with diagrams on the blackboard and the members found it a most practical and useful lecture and accorded Dr Picton a most hearty vote of thanks (Dr Picton's ideas on diet, fresh air and clothing were absolutely in line with modern thinking and well ahead of his time).

Some of the WI's regular commitments have been going on for many years. They regularly receive a letter from Goostrey Rose Day Committee asking whether they would decorate a float or lorry for the Rose Festival. They usually do and have been doing so since the 1920s whenever there has been a festival. A bulb competition in February began in 1922 and continued intermittently until recently. Now, bulbs are planted by members in the village, on many grass verges. In February 1934 a letter was received from a WI in New Zealand, Kaka Point in South Island, suggesting a link between the two institutes. In the 1990s we are still corresponding and visitors from there have visited Goostrey and Goostrey members have visited Kaka Point. When food was short in this country after the Second World War, we received food parcels from Kaka Point.

A drama group, a choir, whist drives, Christmas parties, meals out, celebrations of anniversaries, outings to theatres in various parts of the country, classes in learning skills like painting on china, making Christmas decorations, flower arranging etc, cricket matches against the men of the village, bowling and darts, scrabble competitions, all of these have been enjoyed by Goostrey WI members.\In 1950 various members volunteered to collect information and to help compile a history of the village. This was completed in 1951 and is included in a County Book of the WI, 300 copies of the Goostrey Scrapbook were produced without pictures for local sale. This booklet was reissued a few years ago with the permission of Goostrey WI by the Goostrey Local History Group.

Meetings in July are known as Garden Meetings. Now they are always held in the Village Hall. In the past they were sometimes held in a member's garden and sometimes they were rained off. When they were in members' gardens the hostess often provided ice cream as a treat. Now we always have strawberries and cream and invite representatives from other local WIs to share them with us. Goostrey WI has never done things on a small scale. During the Second World War all local boys serving

Above: Jodrell Side WI members wait to see inside Buckingham Palace, 1995.
Below: Jodrell Side WI

in the forces had received parcels of comforts and the army, navy and air force had received over 200 suitable garments. By the following June, 556 garments had been sent. When more members lived on farms, eggs were collected once a year and taken to various hospitals. Knitting squares, to be made into blankets has been going on for many years, during 1974, 651 squares were knitted and made up into blankets. They went to local hospitals or the WRVS. Recently several blankets have gone to Romania, to keep children and old people warm.

Travelling round Goostrey one sees various gifts given to the village by Goostrey WI on occasions of anniversaries. In 1972 on the 50th anniversary, a village sign was given and erected on the Bog Bean. A seat was donated on Ivy Bank in 1991 and to mark the 75th birthday, a weather vane was erected on the new playing fields. Members also have keepsakes from these anniversaries, such as a white china mug featuring the Goostrey WI badge, small floral china dish etc. We look forward to 2001, the WI's 80th birthday.

JODRELL SIDE WI

IN THE BEGINNING, following the opening of the M6 motorway in 1965, the number of houses and the size of the population of Goostrey rapidly increased. Fire regulations limited the numbers in the old village hall, and there was a long waiting list for new WI members. In March 1970, a preliminary meeting for the formation of a second WI in the village hall was held, and on 15th April 1970 the Goostrey WI record of the meeting states that the new Institute was to be called Jodrell Side. The inaugural meeting of Jodrell Side WI was held in April 1970. Mrs Pownall was elected President, Mrs McNeil was appointed secretary, Mrs M Smith treasurer and 50 members were enrolled. The first night speaker was Mr A W Nicholas of Northwich, on Victorian Porcelain and Mrs Grimsditch won the competition.

Mrs Jose Sykes writes – Our meetings are now held on the second Tuesday evening of each month at the Village Hall in a relaxed and friendly atmosphere. We aim to offer friendship and support and broaden our interests and education with varied speakers, courses and outings. We have a very enthusiastic bowling team, and a popular walking group meeting every month, having explored many places in Cheshire and other counties. One founder member, Blanche Tomkys, still in regular attendance, is a fine example to us all with her energy and enthusiasm, bowling, walking, delivering magazines and attending Group meetings as our representative. We traditionally prepare afternoon tea for the Rose Festival Queen and her entourage. We also contribute to the Cheshire Show and attend National Federation meetings. We are creating an embroidered table cover to commemorate the millennium and our special millennium project is raising funds to provide books for the village school. We are always happy to try new ventures, reflecting the interests of the members and look forward to discovering new friends and activities in the coming years. **GR**

Above: the Chrysanthemum Show, 1964. The Chrysanthemum Society started in 1951.
The top class blooms are well worth viewing each September.
Below: the Chrysanthemum Show, 1999.

GOOSTREY SPORTS

Above: four vicars play an inaugural tennis match in 1907. The courts were on Bridge House grounds, Blackden Lane.

THE TENNIS CLUB officially opened on 17th July 1909. The courts, situated at the rear of Bridge House, Blackden Lane, were first played by the following vicars: Rev C E Muckleston, Rev T M Griffiths, Mr J F T Royds and Rev E Armistead (vicar at that time). Other club members then played, after which a most excellent tea was provided in a tent, presided over by Mrs Locket, Mrs Marlour, Mrs Platt, Miss H Knowles and Mrs Wardleworth. Mrs Egerton-Leigh and Mrs Walters kindly sent gifts of cake for tea and the celebration continued with singing and dancing.

The club met a distinct need in the village and proved to be the envy of many neighbouring parishes, the courts being well laid. Early members included Grace and Margaret Darlington, Mildred Rees, Winnie Entwistle, Annie Blain, May Summerfield, Mary Groves, Joan Maddock, Ada Richard and Percy Knowles, Francis Smallwood, Herbert Edwards, Norman Lever, Ben Lambert, and Robert Cooper. The club was disbanded when too many members were called up to serve in the forces during the 1939-45 war.

In the 1960s a committee was formed in an effort to acquire a playing field, there being no facilities whatsoever for the villagers at this stage. This committee consisted of Mr B Rodgers, Chairman; Mr Tony O'Neill, Treasurer; Mr Malcolm Wright and Mr Colin Smallwood, Secretary. Colin went round to numerous villagers and received several donations so that the committee could make a start. Several functions were held, the main one being the very first Traction Engine Rally at Astle Park, when a grand profit of £802.17s was raised. Support was received from the Cheshire CC

Top: tennis players, 1935. Annie Blain, Harry Tickle, Bessie Blain, Win and Ben Lambert and, seated, Grace Darlington.
Centre: the cricket team in the 1920s in front of the Crown Inn.
Bottom: Goostrey FC, 1906.

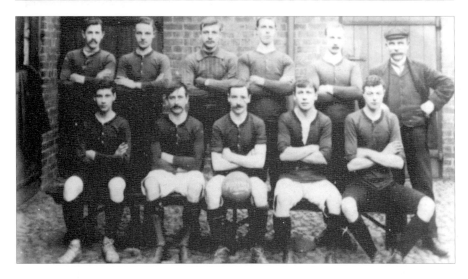

Playing Fields Association, and from the horse shows and gymkhanas held at Hamilton Lodge, by kind permission of Mr David Hunter. A request from the Village Hall Committee suggested that it would be in the best interests of the village if the groups were to join, as a new Village Hall was planned, and thus the Goostrey Village Hall & Playing Fields Committee was formed.

For the next decade or more, nothing was being done regarding playing fields, until newcomers formed the Grass Committee, and after much hard work in the 1990s came the great day on 26th September 1993 a tree was planted by local MP Anne Winterton, on land off Booth Bed Lane for Sports and Recreation. Two years after the official opening, there is a new football pitch, bowling green, tennis courts and hockey (5-a-side), a new pavilion and plans for cricket facilities. *GR*

GOOSTREY WIN THE TIN CUP
Football Club (founded 1903)

A FOOTBALL MATCH was played on 27th May 1906 at the Swan Field, Station Road, Holmes Chapel, when the men of Holmes Chapel opposed the team from Goostrey. The village blacksmith gave a metal cup which he had made, for the winning team. The match was keenly fought and tackles were hard near goal.

The Chapel men scored first, a good shot from Bill Johnson was missed by the goalkeeper from Goostrey. During the second half, the Goostrey men attacked strongly and were given a penalty kick for rough play by a Chapel player and Ryder scored successfully.

Near the end, Goostrey scored a second goal, a pass from George Hamner was put in the goal by Harrison and that was the final score. Mr Broad handed the cup to the

Below: football team, 1947.

Goostrey Select XI v. Manchester City Veterans
This match was played in September 1992 and raised £400 towards
the "Grass" fund to provide village facilities.
Above: Goostrey Select XI, photo © Congleton Chronicle
Below: Manchester City Veterans, photo © Congleton Chronicle

Goostrey team. Also at the game were W Pickford, H Darlington and L Richardson. The Holmes Chapel men were angry to lose and chased the winning team back towards the river Dane after they had grabbed their jackets and the cup but the Goostrey men got over the stream safely.

After the Tin Cup had been on display at the Red Lion Inn, someone placed it in the branches of a pear tree next to the pub, opposite Church Cottages and there it hung for many years!

In 1920 a meeting was held on 20th August to make arrangements for the coming season. The club has been very fortunate in obtaining from Mr Worth, with Mrs Glazebrook's sanction, the use of a field for recreation purposes, where it will be possible to have the football grounds for both seniors and juniors and a railed-in cricket pitch, which can be properly kept and if the present enthusiasm is maintained, there seems no reason why a very flourishing Recreation Club should not become firmly established in the village. The expenses are likely to be considerable but the club has some substantial backing and if our young men, on whose behalf it has been organised, are as keen about it as they appear to be, we are sure that they will not allow the club to languish for lack of funds. T Wardleworth was elected Captain of the football club, T Stonier Vice-Captain and E Bateman Match Secretary. A Selection Committee was appointed and Mr Marlor, who is acting as General Club Secretary, undertook to act as Referee whenever possible. The meeting closed, wishing the club a very successful season and a hope that the weather would prove encouraging for both football and cricket. **GR**

Above: Goostrey AFC, 1962, winners of the East Cheshire League Challenge Cup.

1962 CUP FINAL: GOOSTREY 2 PEOVER 1

The East Cheshire League Challenge Cup went to Goostrey when they scraped to victory on the Carnival Field in Wilmslow. Both teams played a brilliant game but Goostrey had the edge – and the luck.

Up to the last minute no one could have called the winner. The two sides were evenly matched: and there were chances at both ends but it wasn't until the 70th minute that the first goal was chalked up. Goostrey's outside right Frank Hough shot from a narrow angle and the Peover goalkeeper misjudged it – one-nil. Five minutes later Peover had little difficulty in equalising when they were awarded a penalty. Left back Mathias placed his shot well and Goostrey keeper Ryder had little chance for a save.

Level-pegging as the match drew to a climax, Peover hit the post twice. Goostrey's Graham Hulme went off a few minutes before the end with an injured foot yet star striker Hough was able to claim his second goal just before the final whistle and the crowd went wild.

Presenting the Cup the Rev. John Culey, vicar of Holmes Chapel and Chairman of the East Cheshire League said that, because Peover had won the league it was only fitting that Goostrey had won the Cup.

The Goostrey XI were: Ryder, Hammond, Hough, Hulme, Burgess, Wooton, Hough, Bowyer, Collinge, Walker and Wratton.

Above: the new sports and recreation facilities take shape down Booth Bed Lane. Land was acquired in September 1993 for tennis courts, a football pitch, bowling green, 5-a-side hockey pitch etc.
Right: children stage a petition in the 1960s about having no playing field.

GIRLS' CLUB 1920

September 10 1908 – Parish magazine.

Mr & Mrs Egerton Leigh entertained children from Goostrey and Lower Withington School, some older people attended too. After tea, races and various other sports took place, while the elders availed themselves wandering through the large gardens.

Lydia Bagnall, who became Lydia Smallwood, recalled going to this treat. The Goostrey children had walked to Jodrell Hall. They had to take their own cups, had had a lovely day and were presented with 1/- each when they came away.

With the assistance of Miss Armistead and several others who have most kindly promised their help, Miss Marlor is proposing to start a Girls' Club, to meet one evening a week during the winter months. The idea has been eagerly taken up by all who have been consulted and we heartily welcome it. It is proposed to devote the first part of the evening to useful work and instruction in various subjects and the second part to games and amusement. The club is primarily intended for older girls but any over 14 years of age will be eligible for membership. – Parish magazine.

There was also a ladies hockey team in the village from 1920 onwards. **GR**

HORSE RACING

GOOSTREY HAS ALWAYS found people who were keen to organise sports of all kinds, be it the football, tennis or cricket we have covered above. Horse racing was also very well supported.

Captain Dronsfield of Blackden Manor allowed his fields to be used to organise this event annually in order that the Goostrey people could raise funds to purchase a wooden ex-army billet from a government department at Bettisfield in Shropshire. This was transported by local men (Street, Peak and Foden families) etc, all in the building trade, and they were responsible for the erection of the hall, which was officially opened in 1921, where whist drives, dancing and many other functions have been held over the years. Now in 1999 the same hall (renovated several times) is used as the Youth Centre.

The initial upkeep was financed by the profits from the horse racing, which took place from 1921 to 1929 at Blackden Manor, then the site was at Broadway Farm until 1939. Good financial support also came from the Dakins of Blackden Hall, Glazebrooks of Twemlow Hall, Sir Edwin and Lady Stockton of Jodrell Hall and the Goodwin family, who had set up a large fruit farm at the Orchards, Twemlow.

An extract from the *Congleton Chronicle* states that in 1923 the Goostrey Sports and Horse Races were held at Blackden Manor on Saturday July 30. 2,200 paid for

Goostrey
WAKE, 1828.

The Public are respectfully informed, that the ANNUAL FESTIVITIES will commence on Monday the 20th day of October, when FUN, FROLIC, and DIVERSION will take place at the day and bring it lads and lasses fair,
And drive corroding care away.

On MONDAY,

A Purse value £50,
For any horse, mare or gelding, that never started for a £50 Plate. Heats, three times round the course.

GOOSE RIDING,
The winner to have the Goose.

DUCK SWIMMING.

A PIG RACE, the winner to have the Pig.

A BAG RACE,
By Ladies for a handsome Shawl.

Grinning through a Collar,
For a good Cheshire Cheese.

On TUESDAY,

A DONKEY RACE,
For a prime Leg of Mutton. Heats, twice round the course.

GOOSE RIDING. DUCK SWIMMING.

A FOOT RACE,
By Ladies all ages, for Four Yards of good Linen Cloth. Jumping for a pair of Stockings. Prison-Bar Play for 12 Yards of Fashionable Ribbons.

A Bag Race, for a New Hat.

On WEDNESDAY,
A GOOD

Saddle, Bridle and Whip,
By Galloways, (under 14 hands high) Heats, three times round.

A RACE by Boys, for a New Water Proof HAT.

A Pig Race. Goose Riding.

Tea Drinking by 12 of the oldest Women in the Parish, for a pound of 12s. Tea.

BALLS AND ASSEMBLIES EACH NIGHT AS USUAL.

All disputes to be settled by the Committee.

God save the King and all his Subjects.

E. Evans, Printer, Knutsford.

Top left: Mr Worth at Goostrey Races, an annual event between 1921 and 1939.
Centre left: 1920s racegoers
Below left: Congleton band at Goostrey races in the 1930s.
Below right: Colin Smallwood with the 1922 trophy.

admission at the gate and 350 entries were received for the events. Mr J Standeven of Congleton is to be congratulated on securing the Goodwin Challenge Cup and Goostrey Cup with his Anelida.

Somewhere there must be a number of trophies that were presented, and very handsome they were too. One of these has returned to Goostrey through the kindness of Mr Arthur Jarvis of Poynton. The handsome trophy dated 1922, over a foot in height, was presented to rider Frank Jarvis for winning the one mile hurdle race that year. Frank Jarvis had won the cup riding *Moorhen* for Mr Dronsfield.

When the venue was changed to Broadway Farm on Jodrell Road, a public footpath was made available for all the supporters to take from the station to the races. A great deal of financial support was also raised by the Goostrey Football Club, who played soccer at senior cup and league level for the Mid-Cheshire League, Crewe and Macclesfield areas, by holding a weekly Saturday night dance in the hall.

Music was provided by Cath Jones from Sandbach, or the local group, with Alec Newton on piano, Billy Newton on drums, Ted Norbury, violin, Len Ward, accordion, Ted Ryder on guitar, Wish Lambert with a saxophone. All good lively music from 8pm to midnight, admission was a tanner (6d hop), then 1/-. Eventually, due to rising costs it became 2/- then 2/6d, refreshments were usually provided by Mrs Bates, or on some occasions purchased from Mandervilles of Holmes Chapel.

Helpers always included the three Davies sisters, Mrs A T and R Rees, and Violet lloyd and Harriet Sweatman. The football was suspended during the war years, except for some charity games, in aid of the Red Cross etc. after the war competitive football at league level was taken up again until some time around 1963. Now, with the new sports complex, football is played by various age groups. GR

GYMKHANA

FURTHER MONEY WAS raised for the fund between 1964 and 1971 at the horse show and gymkhana held at Hamilton Lodge Allostock, by kind permission of Mr David Hunter. (Goostrey Village Hall and Playing Fields Foundation was formed when the two organisations joined together).

The horse shows and gymkhanas were a great success but several were held in inclement weather. Notwithstanding, they seemed to provide the real spirit of the true country show. Records were broken in 1968 when more than 2,000 people attended the event. Some of the finest horses in the area were gathered together for the varied programme of events.

It was not all horses however, as dogs attracted much attention in one section of the arena. There were also Morris Dancing and children's dancing displays, a fun fair and Punch & Judy show, then a dance in Goostrey Village Hall to round off the day. Goostrey WI organised the refreshments and John Lawton, licensee of the Crown, ran

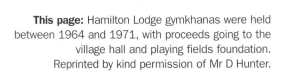

This page: Hamilton Lodge gymkhanas were held between 1964 and 1971, with proceeds going to the village hall and playing fields foundation. Reprinted by kind permission of Mr D Hunter.

the bar. Goostrey Morris Dancers organised a draw. The Methodist Youth Club members manned the sweet stall, while bowls, tombola and a treasure hunt were other attractions There were a number of trophies to be won. The coveted *Daily Express* National Foxhunter Competition was a highlight each year along with other trophies. In 1967, a fire broke out at one of the Hamilton Lodge stables. At the height of the blaze one of the stable girls braved the flames and rescued several ponies and a hunter. She was awarded the silver medallion and certificate from the RSPCA. The award was made at the 1967 Gymkhana. **GR**

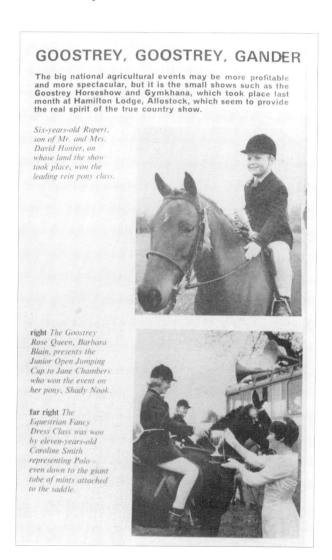

GOOSTREY, GOOSTREY, GANDER

The big national agricultural events may be more profitable and more spectacular, but it is the small shows such as the Goostrey Horseshow and Gymkhana, which took place last month at Hamilton Lodge, Allostock, which seem to provide the real spirit of the true country show.

Six-years-old Rupert, son of Mr. and Mrs. David Hunter, on whose land the show took place, won the leading rein pony class.

right *The Goostrey Rose Queen, Barbara Blain, presents the Junior Open Jumping Cup to Jane Chambers who won the event on her pony, Shady Nook.*

far right *The Equestrian Fancy Dress Class was won by eleven-years-old Caroline Smith representing Polo – even down to the giant tube of mints attached to the saddle.*

JODRELL BANK

Right: "Helicopter Rescues Jodrell Bank Hat Box, 1961". Eight minutes work by two men and a helicopter saved Sir Bernard Lovell and his team of scientists a week's work, when a test pilot flew his helicopter 100 feet above the lip of the telescope, letting down a sling and picking up the central "square box" – a transmitter weighing 3cwt.
Below: construction of Jodrell Bank Radio Telescope, completed in 1957.

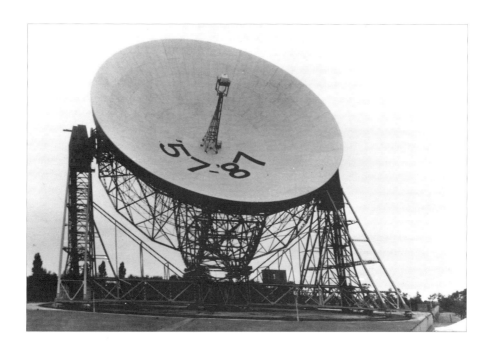

Above: Jodrell Bank's 30th anniversary.
Below: a postcard of Jodrell Bank.

Above: a visitor "tunes in", part of the interactive visitors" centre.

PARISH COUNCIL CENTENARY

Above: a Service of Thanksgiving on the 100th Anniversary of Goostrey Parish Council in 1994 was followed by a civic reception in the old school hall. The centenary cake (below) was made by Mrs E Simpson and decorated by Mrs J Turner.
Pictured above are (left to right) the Mayor and Mayoress of Congleton, Parish Chairman Jonathan Robinson, Mrs Anne Winterton MP, Mrs Geoffrey Turner, Mr Nicholas Winterton MP, Rt. Rev. Geoffrey Turner, Bishop of Stockport

RECENT DEVELOPMENTS

Above: new bungalows on Sandy Lane.
Below: starter homes, 1998.

OPENING THE OLD FOOTPATH

The footpath group made an old public path accessible by making a walkway at a trouble spot. The ceremonial tape was cut by the Mayor of Congleton with scissors provided by sponsors Manchester Airport Community Trust Fund.

GOOSTREY TALES

TRAVELLERS

RAGE & BONE MEN would come around the village with a horse and cart and, if you gave them anything, you could have either a few pennies, a donkey stone or a goldfish in a jam jar. Gypsies also called selling clothes pegs and posies, and would have lucky sprigs of heather. Their baskets would be covered over with brightly coloured shawls. men with turbans would also call, opening big suitcases full of wares. They usually came round on Sandbach market day (Tuesday).

OLDEST MAN

IN 1908 THE funeral of Mr Henry Clarke of Cedar Lodge, Main Road is recorded, at that time the oldest inhabitant of Goostrey (aged 92). He worked from the age of eight for Mr Egerton Leigh of Jodrell Hall, later becoming bailiff for the Leighs' property in 1866, remaining there until he retired in 1905. He came from a long lived family and it is believed his grandfather lived to be 112 – probably Goostrey's oldest resident.

GOOSTREY AT WAR

WITH THE CALL-UP of Goostrey men in 1914, many women went to work on the land. Mrs Voss of Goostrey had notice from the Board of Agriculture that clothing was available at low prices: shirts 5/3d, knickerbockers 2/-, overalls 5/11d, leather nailed boots 7/8d, leggings 4/-, hats 11d and sou-westers 1/5d.

The Cenotaph bears the names of those brave men who died in action, including Major Philip Glazebrook of Twemlow Hall and Captain Thomas Rufus of The Ash, Goostrey who was posthumously awarded the Military Cross.

The 1939-45 war years in Goostrey were much the same as in many villages, with the arrival from Manchester of evacuees, some never having seen cows or sheep before and not knowing that chestnuts grew on trees. They were billeted in homes wherever a spare room was available and a few stayed until the end of the war.

Women came to replace men on the land and there was the formation of the Goostrey Home Guard, the auxiliary fire service and ARP voluntary fire watchers on duty each night. Bombs did fall locally and several farm buildings were damaged. Mrs Coddington from the White House organised knitting parties, making woollen scarves, gloves, socks etc. for the forces and distributing them far and wide. Food parcels were also sent wherever possible. The village retains a strong connection with the British Legion. **GR**

PAST & PRESENT VILLAGERS

Lydia Smallwood, Freda Bailey,
Tim Cumberbirch

Clement and Annie Dakin.

Doris Colclough circa 1920.

Edward Simpson, Fred Lloyd
and Martin Leake.

Goostrey Grannies

J H Blurton

Polly Wilkinson

PAST & PRESENT VILLAGERS

Albert Groves and Sally.

Robert Duckworth.

Dr. Lionel Picton.

1900. George Hamner Senior, his day's work done, walks home from the Wood Lane area towards Sandy Lane and Booth Bed Lane (the latter being just a track with no buildings). To the right in the distance is the only house visible, Holly Bank, a farm on the Main Road (now no. 65). The only building in Sandy Lane is not visible. The original large framed photograph belongs to Miss M Hooley.